For Love of Ukraine

SHARYN L. BORODINA

YWAM Publishing is the publishing ministry of Youth With A Mission (YWAM), an international missionary organization of Christians from many denominations dedicated to presenting Jesus Christ to this generation. To this end, YWAM has focused its efforts in three main areas: (1) training and equipping believers for their part in fulfilling the Great Commission (Matthew 28:19), (2) personal evangelism, and (3) mercy ministry (medical and relief work).

To learn more about our books and materials, call (425) 771-1153 or (800) 922-2143 or email books@ywampublishing.com. Visit us online at www.ywampublishing.com.

For Love of Ukraine: A Story of Faith, Family, and the Fight for Freedom
Copyright © 2025 by Sharyn L. Borodina

Published by YWAM Publishing
a ministry of Youth With A Mission
P.O. Box 55787, Seattle, WA 98155-0787

All rights reserved. No part of this book may be reproduced in any form without permission in writing from the publisher, except in the case of brief quotations embodied in critical articles or reviews.

Library of Congress Cataloging-in-Publication Data — Pending

ISBN 978-164836-157-9 (paperback)

Unless otherwise noted, all Scripture quotations are taken from the Holy Bible, New International Version®, NIV®. Copyright © 1973, 1978, 1984, 2011 by Biblica, Inc.™ Used by permission of Zondervan. All rights reserved worldwide. www.zondervan.com. The "NIV" and "New International Version" are trademarks registered in the United States Patent and Trademark Office by Biblica, Inc.™

Verses marked NKJV are taken from the New King James Version®. Copyright © 1982 by Thomas Nelson. Used by permission. All rights reserved.

First printing 2025

Printed in the United States of America

Trust in the L*ORD with all your heart,*
And lean not on your own understanding;
In all your ways acknowledge Him,
and He shall direct your paths.

—Proverbs 3:5–6 NKJV

I dedicate this book to all the prayer warriors, ministry partners, friends, and family who have walked alongside our family and our ministry for almost three decades. You have held us up and rooted us on. We are more grateful for your presence in our lives than words can say.

Ruslan, Gloria, and Emily, thank you for trusting me to write your story too. You are my greatest gifts this side of heaven.

To my parents, David and Sandra Magers, thank you for letting me fly to far off places, and for creating a home that has always been my safe harbor.

To my heavenly Father, all glory goes to you! May our history reflect first and foremost HIS story in our lives.

The darker gray area in eastern Ukraine, as of publishing, was the front line or hot zone of the Russia-Ukraine War.

Contents

Artwork sent from a US elementary school to encourage Ukrainian children, Tesco Refugee Center, Przemyśl, Poland, April 2022

Foreword

You are about to get a personal, gritty, heartfelt tour of one of the major hot spots on Earth. You will not be sitting on a couch listening to accounts of the war in Ukraine. You will be driving down the road, sometimes just hours ahead of closures of borders. You will experience what few get to feel because you will see these things through the eyes of a young Ukrainian who loves his country and the eyes of a girl from Idaho who takes us with her as she learns a new language and culture and falls in love with this land. You will also see it through the eyes of their children as they experience war firsthand and ask, "Why?"

I got to know Sharyn and Ruslan early on in the story. They came to our Leadership Training School in Kyiv in 2002 along with 120 others who were excited about the huge possibilities of the newly liberated country of Ukraine. In the midst of all the opportunities and wonderful freedom we all felt at that time, none of us knew what lay ahead and the cost that would have to be paid for that freedom.

If ever there was a person "called to the Kingdom for such a time as this," it is Sharyn. At the beginning of the war, Sharyn shared with me her heart for the staff who were serving around the clock, rescuing little babushkas from basements where they were hiding, taking food and supplies to the towns and villages devastated by the war. It was her vision to have a place where the helpers could go to be ministered to. It wasn't just the staff that received that ministry, countless pastors and missionaries came. It didn't stop there, and it has not stopped as Sharyn continues to minister in some amazingly creative ways.

I am so glad that you get to read this story. It's a tragic yet wonderful story of God's leading, his mercy and grace in the midst of difficulties, and his love poured out through his children. Sharyn does a wonderful job of taking us with her on this tour of Ukraine.

—Al Akimoff, YWAM Slavic Ministries

PROLOGUE

Just a Little Miracle Story

Writing this book has been a remarkable journey of personal growth. As with any first-time undertaking, I've wondered if I'm a good enough writer to be published. I've doubted myself, prayed, and listened to the Lord. His word to me was "Write this story."

In 2022 the urgency to get the book done became more intense. It was as if the Lord was saying, "Write this story…NOW!!!" So after many years of trying to carve out a consistent writing schedule, I parked myself at a coffee shop three times a week and wrote until the first draft was complete.

Presenting a manuscript to a publishing house as a first-time author is an act of faith in and of itself. When YWAM Publishing agreed to take on this project, I was amazed. Eager for feedback, I waited expectantly for their editor to come on board. I was excited to work together to make the book even better.

In late February 2024, I received the long-awaited email from YWAM editor Scott Tompkins. Scott's first few paragraphs summarized his experience in YWAM and his work history as an editor. My thought right away was *Wow, YWAM Publishing has given me the Cadillac of editors.* As I read on, Scott's email listed all the things he felt needed to be improved in the storyline. It was clear that if he was going to take the project, he and I would need to work closely together to make significant changes.

What can I say, I didn't handle that constructive criticism quite as well as I had hoped I might. Again, I started to doubt. I also wondered where I was going to find the extra hours to work with this editor to get the book up to his expectations!

Lord, I prayed, *maybe we don't need to go this route. Maybe I'm not a good enough writer. Are you sure this book is supposed to be published this way? Lord, would you show me please if this is the editor I'm supposed to work with?*

Scott and I had made an appointment to have our first meeting via Zoom the following week, and I asked God to give me the confirmation I was looking for between now and then.

A few days before our appointment, my husband, Ruslan, and I received an email from our good friend Mark Tremper. We go way back with Mark and his wife, Karen, and we were excited that in just over a month Mark was coming to volunteer with us in Ukraine. His message brimmed with enthusiasm:

> I need to tell you that I've just had a very interesting conversation with my best friend. We've been close for over 40 years, and Karen and I actually named one of our sons after him. I was telling him about my upcoming trip to Ukraine, and about the amazing connection we have with you guys. I told him that 30 years ago, we were on a YWAM outreach to Ukraine where we met this Ukrainian youth who had been invited to an informal Bible study. A few weeks later, Karen led him to the Lord. Two years after that his future wife came through a YWAM school that Karen and I were staffing. Karen was her leader in that school. Her outreach was in Ukraine, and that is where they met and fell in love. Now three decades later I get to go back to Ukraine and work with their ministry. It's such a "God connection" we have with them!

At this point, Mark's best friend interrupted him.

"Mark, I'm pretty sure I just finished reading that story!"

"You're kidding!"

"No, are the names of this couple by any chance Ruslan and Sharyn?"

"Yes!"

As it turns out, my YWAM Publishing editor was the same Scott Tompkins who had influenced Mark's life for more than forty years. Scott and his wife, Sandi, were one of two couples who long ago encouraged Mark and Karen to take a Youth With A Mission course called the Crossroads Discipleship Training School (CDTS). The Trempers did the school in Montana, and their CDTS outreach trip took them to Ukraine. There they met a young man named Ruslan, and ultimately that meeting led to the story you are now holding in your hands.

As I absorbed Mark's story, I realized that God had not just sent me a YWAM editor, he had sent me the man who helped put into motion our entire story.

I asked God for confirmation, and boy did I get it. So did Scott! Only God could have connected us to work together on a story that Scott was already part of, even though we hadn't known it!

CHAPTER 1

Rooted in Ukraine

A few years ago, my family and I had the pleasure of spending a day in the redwood forests of Northern California. Among the giant sequoia and California redwoods are the tallest and biggest trees on our planet. Our first hike of the day, Lady Bird Johnson Grove Trail, left me speechless! Walking beneath the canopy of some of the largest and oldest trees in the world was an experience like nothing I've ever known. I felt so small, so insignificant as I stepped through a carpet of light-green ferns that make their home amidst these beautiful giants. This was one of God's special places, and we delighted in our discovery!

We walked along the trails, breathing in the aroma of the forest. Our girls skipped along fallen tree trunks so thick I worried they might fall off and hurt themselves. As I looked up, the trees seemed to never end. I noticed with quiet captivation the way the sun cast its glistening beams down through the treescapes, down to where its rays warmed our faces.

It was a surprise to discover that the pine cone of these gigantic trees is about the size of an olive, yet it produces trees that can grow more than three hundred feet tall! That's higher than a thirty-five-story building! A full-grown Redwood can weigh 1.7 million pounds, and one harvested tree can produce enough lumber to build twenty-five medium-sized houses! With one of these tiny cones nestled in my hand, I stood at the foot of the largest tree I had ever seen. I thought about how inconsequential this little tree seed was, yet nestled in my hand was unbelievable potential.

I imagined how deep the root systems of such a tree must be in order to keep something so tall and heavy upright. We were fascinated to discover that in fact their root systems reach only about ten to twelve feet beneath the ground. These giants stay upright through storms, pestilence, and floods by interlocking with the roots of other redwood trees. The roots of one tree can spread out over an acre of land, up to one hundred feet in every direction. The trees are a community, holding on to one another, holding each other up, with interlocking roots stretching out for miles. Together they lend their strength to help each other stand tall, come what may, through the tests of time.

The people of Ukraine are very much like a redwood tree. They live in a land with a long history and great potential, even if much of the world knew little about Ukraine until recently. Theirs is a history fraught with incredible challenges and hardships. Yet together, by God's grace and with the support of many, many people who have been called to walk alongside them, Ukraine still is. Their people, culture, heritage, and legacy still stand.

Ukrainians have been fighting to survive for centuries. Because of their rich black soils, strategic seaports, and location as a borderland between the East and West, Ukraine has been invaded by the Romans, Turks, Hungarians, Germans, and most recently the Russians.

The nation was at peace when I first visited as an American teenager on a mission for Jesus. It had recently been freed from the seventy-year grip of the Soviet Union, but the signs of cruel Communist rule were everywhere. During that trip, God planted within me a love for these tough and resilient Slavic people. I eventually married one, and I became a permanent resident of Ukraine, sharing in its joys and sorrows.

I first set foot in Ukraine on my nineteenth birthday, March 25, 1996. On that day I not only caught my first glimpses of this country that would change my life, but I also met the man I would one day marry. I've thanked the Lord many times for marking my life calendar with these two momentous and inseparable occasions.

Since then, my roots have been intertwined with those of Ukraine. Here, God has nourished me in Christian community—community we've been able to extend to others who need Jesus. Here, God has graciously used me to answer the prayers of others, while sending others to minister to me.

Over the years, I've probably been asked at least once per week, "Why on earth would you choose to live here?" Even in times of peace, there were many Ukrainians who would have loved the opportunity to move to the United States. The truth is that there isn't a logical answer. I just love this country. I love the people of this country. I love living in this country. I choose to live and work in Ukraine, not because I have to or because it's always easy, but because more than twenty-five years ago, on March 25, God gifted me a smidgen of his love for Slavic peoples. It has never rubbed off even a little. Isn't that amazing!

With love comes joy and also sorrow.

Our daughters and I were out of the country when full-scale war broke out in February 2022, but my husband, Ruslan, was home. As with millions of other Ukrainians, our lives turned upside down. We talked by phone about frightening possibilities, about thoughts you never imagined thinking, about scenarios for which you never thought you'd have to prepare. What if our house is bombed? What if Ternopil is invaded? How can we help the refugees flooding into our city? What if cell and internet services are lost? If we lose communication, how will we find each other?

"Honey," I asked Ruslan, "at what point should you leave, if the situation gets worse? When can you get out, even for a day or two, so we can see you?"

A long silence followed my questions.

"Sharyn, leaving right now just isn't an option," Ruslan finally answered. "There's too much happening, and I'm needed here. You know you and the girls mean everything to me. We must trust that the Lord will lead us through this."

I knew Ruslan was right. While the tragedy and uncertainty unleashed by Russia's full-scale invasion was far beyond anything we had experienced before, this wasn't the first time that Ruslan and I had needed to trust God in difficult circumstances. Over the decades, God had patiently taught us that we needed to trust him each day. Every single day. And this day our Youth With A Mission training center in Ternopil was flooded with refugees headed west toward Ukraine's border with Poland, Hungary, Romania, and Slovakia. Hundreds were sleeping on our floors and receiving whatever aid our staff could give them.

When I asked how he and our team were doing, Ruslan replied, "We're holding it together. There are people everywhere. And not just people—dogs, cats, birds, our base is a zoo. It's amazing, though, the way the community is coming together to help. Tonight one of the restaurants in town brought us sushi for dinner. People from all over the city are volunteering to help, but the need is just incredible."

"What are you hearing from people coming through?" I asked.

"You can tell what city people are coming from just by looking at them. Kharkiv, Chernihiv, Mariupol, they are so traumatized, they can barely function. People have lost everything. They don't know what to do, where to go. They are beyond exhausted. We found a psychologist today who is going to try to help some of the most traumatized."

As my husband worked hard in Ukraine, my teenage daughters and I worked hard on a new mission, mobilizing Christians worldwide toward prayer and support for Ukraine. We set up a ministry hub in Kraków, Poland, and helped coordinate relief funds coming through a variety of YWAM and church giving sites. The circumstances were newly daunting, heartbreaking. Yet as before, the question before me remained the same: "Lord, can I trust you?"

Growing up in rural Idaho, I never dreamed I would call a war zone home. I never dreamed I would be displaced from what had been my life. But here I am. Throughout history, how many millions have found themselves in a situation in which they didn't expect to be—where honestly they didn't want to be? At some point, in some way or another, isn't this an experience every one of us encounters? What then? To what—or whom—can we turn?

For me in this season, prayer has become more than just a conversation with God, it has become a lifeline, especially when anxious thoughts try to steal away my peace. Often, I fall asleep praying for this land that I love. I pray for protection of the soldiers on the battlefield, especially that every soldier would have an opportunity to receive Jesus as their Lord and Savior. I pray for the widows and orphans, for those who have lost close family members in this awful war. I pray for our Youth With A Mission staff and volunteers, many of whom are ministering in dangerous places.

I pray for the broken ones—the amputees and the former POWs, many of whom were starved and tortured in Russian prisons. I pray for physical healing, but the greater need is often for emotional healing from trauma. I pray for the Russians too, also beloved by God, that they would see the truth and have the courage to fight against the evil of their government and bring the war to an end.

This is my frequent prayer: *Lord, have mercy. You go before us; you are the God who is mighty in battle. Please bring peace to this nation. Bring your victory and hope for Ukraine.*

As I tell you my story, I don't know the next chapters for my family or for Ukraine.

In this time of great upheaval, I sometimes find myself looking back. My dreams take me back to the time I first came to love this place and its people. To the time when Ukraine became the place I call home.

In awe of the magnificent redwoods:
The Borodin family, 2019

CHAPTER 2

The Call to Missions

I'm not sure where it came from, the sense of adventure inside me. From my earliest years I just wanted to explore, and my north Idaho backyard was an amazing place to wander. My little gang of neighborhood friends and I would travel the countryside on our dirt bikes, scouting out each forested hill, creek, and pond. From one side of Priest Lake, Idaho, to the other, I grew up swimming, waterskiing, boating, and trekking. I took pride in being able to do anything any guy could do.

In my high school years, I dreamed of joining the Air Force or the Peace Corps. I looked at study abroad programs that would take me to the Amazon jungle or the mountains of Tibet. This surprised my parents, David and Sandy Magers, since there were no world travelers in our family. Our radius of influence didn't go much farther than Spokane, Washington, which was one hundred miles away. Yet I knew I wanted to experience more than what my beautiful north Idaho had to offer.

My first taste of the world beyond north Idaho came the summer before my sophomore year of high school when I learned about a program called Youth Attack. This summer program for teenagers was being run by an organization called Youth With A Mission—or, for short, YWAM (pronounced

Why-Wham). We would be given a few days of missions training in Montana, then head out on a ten-day outreach trip to Tijuana, Mexico.

As soon as I heard about this program, I knew I wanted to do it. I cared a lot about my relationship with Jesus and was excited to be a missionary for a couple of weeks. What drew me the most, however, was the opportunity to see a different place and encounter different people. I was curious about the world outside Idaho.

Of course, I needed permission to go. My mom, a nurse by profession, had traded in her stethoscope for motherhood in her early thirties when I was born. She loved being a homemaker for my dad, me, and later my two brothers, Robbie and Corey. My dad was the local law enforcement officer in our area, working for the U.S. Forest Service. I grew up with police officers stopping in and Dad getting called out in the middle of the night. We all would listen for his call sign, 480, on the police radio that was always on in our kitchen. Dad would often introduce me to his friends as his pride and joy, which both embarrassed me and made me feel special and loved. He was very protective of me, and I was astonished when he gave the go-ahead for the Mexico trip.

I think he gave his blessing because he was certain I wouldn't be able to raise the required five hundred dollars. When I did raise the funds, Dad used his most intimidating policeman voice over the phone to question the group leader, Deb Possien. He said he would hold her personally responsible if anything happened to me in Tijuana. Years later, Deb admitted that she might have prayed harder for me than for other students on that trip!

After three days of training at the YWAM campus in Lakeside, Montana, our team boarded an old Greyhound bus and embarked on the two-day drive to Tijuana. That trip left a deep impression on me. In San Diego, California, we passed some of the richest neighborhoods I had ever seen. Just a few miles south, we crossed the Mexico border and entered the slums of Tijuana. House after house was built from scraps of plywood, cardboard, and metal. I had never seen such poverty, and I didn't understand how such wealth could exist right next door to such need. Yet the people I met were not miserable. They were so happy and thankful that we had come to help build a church in their village. They welcomed us and showered us with whatever hospitality they could.

I will never forget the promise I made to God toward the end of our time of ministry in this village. I was looking out over the Pacific Ocean, just a few blocks away from the wall that separated the USA from Mexico.

God, I don't know what you have for me in my life, but whatever I do, I want to help people like this. I want to help people who have so little, and I want to share with them the hope of Jesus.

It was a holy promise—the heartfelt prayer of conviction from a fifteen-year-old—and the first step toward a calling that would set the course for my entire life.

Three years later I returned to the Lakeside base for a YWAM Discipleship Training School (DTS). It was February 1996, and I entered our snow-covered dormitory eager to see what God had for me in this five-month-long course.

"To know God and make him known" is the theme of every DTS. First, students hear from speakers on topics like the father heart of God, a biblical worldview, intercession, relationships, and evangelism. Then, during the outreach portion of the course, usually in a foreign land, these enthusiastic short-term missionaries apply the principles learned in the classroom. Simply put, YWAM aims to share the redeeming power of Jesus with a hurting world.

On this day, as I hurried out to the lecture hall for morning classes, I was met by a blast of frigid air and snow. Though winter was no stranger to me, I couldn't help but look forward to our outreach, which we had heard would take place in sunny South America. I hoped it would be close to a beach.

Imagine my shock when our DTS leaders informed us that we were not going to South America—but to Central and Eastern Europe. They said they had asked God to show them specifically where he wanted us to go on outreach, instead of just picking the spot and then asking him to bless our efforts. They said they had received "a word from the Lord," which was a new concept for me. One of the leaders explained, "During a time of prayer, we all clearly heard the Lord say we were to go to Ukraine, Austria, and the Czech Republic."

I left our morning classes feeling anything but excited about this turn of events. Europe wasn't a part of the world that had ever been on my radar, and quite frankly, I thought our DTS leaders might have been tuned in to the wrong frequency! I was amazed at this idea that through prayer we could hear God speak to us and give specific direction to our plans and purposes. While I didn't doubt God, I wasn't ready to trust that our leaders had heard him correctly.

The new plan was that half the team would go to Ukraine and the other half to Austria. Then we would meet up in the Czech Republic during the second month. I was asked to pray about joining the team going to Ukraine.

God, I have never even heard of this place called Ukraine. Are you sure they got it right? Maybe it was Uruguay. You know, I spent three years studying Spanish in high school, but I don't speak a word of whatever it is they speak in Ukraine. I hear they eat a lot of beets and cabbage there, and I don't especially like beets and cabbage. I'm not picky; I'll go anywhere you send me on the South American continent. But Eastern Europe? Lord, it's cold there in the spring! There are Communists there, whatever that is. This wasn't the plan!

I had just finished reading *Is That Really You, God?* by Loren Cunningham, the founder of YWAM, and that phrase kept going through my mind on that wintry Montana day: "Is that really you, God?" Trust and submission are disciplines that take time and experience to master. The question before me was whether I trusted the Lord enough to lead me down a path that was different from the one I had imagined for myself. Was I going to allow Jesus to be the author of my life? Would I essentially submit the reins to him, and just follow where he might lead me?

Looking back, I can see that this decision was a defining moment for me. What if I had said no? What if I hadn't been able to take that leap of faith, trusting that this God I loved was big enough, faithful enough, and loving enough to handle all the unknowns of my future with confident surety?

This might have been the first time in my walk with Jesus that I truly surrendered to his will, and that decision set the stage for a series of events that would alter my life forever.

Priest Lake, Idaho, from the Magers house

The Magers family: Sandra, Robbie, and Sharyn (standing)
Corey and David (seated), 1991

Sharyn and YWAM Youth Attack Leader Mariska Buzzard on outreach in Tijuana, 1993

Sharyn and Liberty Williams "hanging out" of the bus that took the Youth Attack team roundtrip from Lakeside, Montana, to Baja, California, 1993

CHAPTER 3

We're Not in Kansas Anymore, Toto

March 25, 1996, is a day I will never forget. It was my nineteenth birthday, and as our plane touched down amidst the pink hues of an early morning sunrise, I couldn't help but think it would be a memorable one. After more than thirty hours of travel, my team of seventeen young people had finally landed at the Boryspil International Airport outside of Kyiv, Ukraine. I stepped out of the airplane onto the cracked concrete slabs of the runway and felt a little like Dorothy in *The Wizard of Oz.*

We're not in Kansas anymore, Toto, I thought. But instead of finding a colorful yellow brick road, I had entered a world that felt dark and foreboding. People didn't smile. There was no spark in their eyes or spring to their steps. As we made our way on foot across the runway into the airport, our backpack-toting group from New Zealand, Australia, Norway, Germany, Switzerland, Brazil, Canada, and the USA looked like an in-color portrait in an all-gray world. We were obviously out of place in these surroundings, and I could feel all the eyes following our steps.

Those first impressions of Ukraine were unsettling—so was the immediate, stark realization that this was a country starved of hope. God, in his great love for the people of this nation, had directed our path, so we might do something about changing the hopelessness here.

After making it through customs, we piled our backpacks in the middle of the empty arrival area between the airport exit and the stairs leading down to the toilets, and we tucked ourselves in for a seven-hour wait. Our interpreter would be arriving later with another YWAM team on their way back to Montana. After that group's departure, the interpreter would join us for the six-hour bus ride to a town in western Ukraine called Lutsk.

Hours later, as I awoke with a kink in my neck and the feeling that I would pay big money for a hot shower and the opportunity to change my clothes, I wondered what the Lord had in store for me here.

A month earlier, one of my DTS leaders had come up to me after a time of intercessory prayer. "Sharyn," he said, "I feel like the Lord is saying that something is going to happen during your outreach in Ukraine that is either going to make you want to stay there or lead to your returning again. Be ready—God is about to change your life!"

No pressure there, I thought. Yet as I sat in the airport with my team and pondered what I might experience in this foreign land, I couldn't help but raise my face to the unknown and smile expectantly. My heart had changed toward this trip. I no longer felt that God was forcing me to do something I would hate; my heart was filled with love and compassion for a people I had no connection to at all. I was sold out with the desire to allow the Lord to use me in any way he could—if it meant bringing these precious people into the knowledge of his incredible love and purpose for them.

As our charter bus pulled out of the airport for the six-hour drive to Lutsk, I looked out onto a world that felt like something from the pages of a *National Geographic* magazine. In the forested countryside, small villages buzzed with life. I noticed many old grannies, faces full of wrinkles, digging in gardens or guiding their geese down the roadways. These work-hardened women wore thick boots and layers of clothing that included knee-length dresses, black wool vests, and bright kerchiefs.

In contrast, as we entered Kyiv, the Ukrainian capital, young women walked about in miniskirts, fur coats, and knee-high leather boots. As we passed through the city, I was struck by all the apartment buildings. They looked as if they were constructed of identical gray LEGO blocks, with the windows, balconies, and ground-floor entrances all arranged in similar patterns. Missing were creative elements like color, decor, or landscaping.

I didn't know if this monochrome sameness was for economic or cultural reasons or if it was due to government repression. Whatever the case, not one single thing about these places felt warm or inviting.

Outside Kyiv, as we journeyed on, the villages held a certain charm for me. Each homestead we passed included a small barn within a fenced-in area and a little cottage with four stucco walls, an asbestos roof, and a red brick chimney. Nearly every bit of available land was tilled and ready for the first seeds of spring to be tucked into the dark black soil. Farm animals wandered around everywhere I looked. Peddlers sat in front of their homes selling fresh eggs and milk, plus whatever vegetables or canned preserves they had to spare. Between the villages were vast communal farms that had once produced so much wheat that the area was known as the breadbasket of Eastern Europe.

This picture of the Ukrainian peasantry was both beautiful and unsettling. Beautiful, because it looked like something out of a fairytale that existed hundreds of years ago. Unsettling, because as charming as it was, I couldn't ignore the poverty and depression that hung like a blanket over the land.

We were joined on our bus ride by several members of the youth group we would be working with through our host church, and I was eager to get to know them. I had found a little book on conversational Ukrainian, and as I tried to practice the few sentences I had learned, it quickly became apparent that they weren't going to be enough.

One young man, named Sergei, with a shy smile and kind eyes, motioned for me to follow him to the front of the bus, where our interpreter was sitting. The other four members of the youth group followed him. With six sets of inquisitive eyes all looking at me, I listened as these would-be new friends said something in Ukrainian to our interpreter.

When the interpreter turned to look at me, I found myself staring into the most beautiful, crystal-clear blue eyes I had ever seen. Motioning for me to sit down, he introduced himself. "Hi. My name's Ruslan, and my friends think you're really cool. They want to ask you a few questions, and I'd be happy to interpret for you."

Off we went, all talking and getting to know each other as our bus sped down the bumpy Ukrainian highway. After a while, there was no need to interpret for the others anymore, and Ruslan and I just continued talking in English.

Those moments were the very first in my ongoing love story with Eastern Europe, Slavic peoples, and a special interpreter named Ruslan Borodin.

Sharyn (center) with DTS teammates at YWAM Lakeside, 1996

Some of the YWAM outreach team and local youth at the sanatorium where we were living, Lutsk, Ukraine, 1996 (Ruslan and Sharyn are in the center)

CHAPTER 4

A Bible, a Cowboy, and a Tract

At first glance, Ruslan Volodymyrovych Borodin could have been the model for one of the Soviet propaganda posters. He had that look. Young, handsome, intelligent, squarish head full of thick sandy-brown hair. His engaging blue eyes flashed warmly as he spoke, but they also reflected the pain of his generation. Like many young Ukrainians, Ruslan had suffered the wounds of a childhood marked by alcoholism, divorce, and paternal abandonment. Like too many children, he had roamed the streets while his single mom worked to support the family.

Over a steaming cup of tea in the lobby of the aging health sanatorium where our outreach team was staying, Ruslan told me pieces of his story.

"My mother remarried when I was nine. She had a good job with the military, so we were better off than most people, but life in Ukraine still came with many difficulties. I had dreams of being a professional soccer player, but my mother nudged me toward university studies, specifically languages. I was studying English and German at the university the first time I saw an American."

"So did you have any Christian influence in your life while growing up?"

Ruslan paused to consider my question. "Not really. During the days when Ukraine was part of the Soviet Union, the Christian church didn't have much influence on families. I wasn't aware of the persecution of the church, and I had very little knowledge of what a Bible was, let alone that it was illegal to have one. Still, it was a big surprise when my stepfather brought a Bible home. It fit in the palm of his hand. Out of curiosity, I picked it up and began to read it. It was a New Testament and Psalms edition, the first Bible I had ever touched."

"So what happened when you started reading it?"

"As I started to read, it was like this new life came over me that I had never thought about or experienced before. It felt like fresh air filling me up. As I read, I realized that this was something that I wanted to know more about, but I didn't know how to open the door to it. I felt like I was looking through a keyhole at something beautiful, but I didn't have the key."

While Ruslan was a first-year university student in Lutsk, God used another unlikely person to draw him to Christ—a cattle rancher from Roundup, Montana, named Clay Bedford.

Ruslan explained how he and this rancher had come to cross paths. "Clay later told me that he was at a spiritual crossroads in his life when he heard a speaker from YWAM named David Graham give a message on the father heart of God. It moved him to fully commit his life to Christ and eventually to sign up for a Crossroads DTS at the Lakeside, Montana, base. Months later, on his outreach to Ukraine, I met Clay while he was handing out Christian leaflets and using the only three words of Ukrainian he knew: *'Veez'meet' bood'laska'* — 'Take it please.'"

Ruslan and I laughed because that was about the extent of my Ukrainian vocabulary at this point, but I saw clearly how God used Clay through the simple act of handing Ruslan a tract.

"Yes, I was in the central market shopping for a pair of tennis shoes when I noticed a group of young people standing around this guy. When I learned he was an American, I saw it as an opportunity to practice my English. I accepted the tract from Clay and his invitation to come to a Bible study where I could meet more of his friends from America."

Ruslan said that as he walked home, he read the scripture leaflet Clay had given him, and he felt an immediate desire to attend the Bible study.

Yet something held him back—something internal, and scary, that seemed to scream at him to stay away. "But I knew I needed to go. I was supposed to meet these people and maybe discover if it was possible to know this God in a personal way."

Now I was leaning forward on a hard wooden chair eager to hear what happened next.

"Three days later, on a Saturday evening, I took a twenty-minute walk to the sanatorium where Clay's team was staying. As I turned up the path to their building, I saw a group of foreigners hanging out on the front steps. They welcomed me, and I soon became fast friends with those Jesus-loving English speakers. They openly shared their lives with me and displayed a peace and joy I'd never experienced before."

Three weeks after meeting Clay, Ruslan accepted his new friends' invitation to follow Christ.

As I sipped my tea, I marveled at the story I'd just heard. A smuggled Bible, a cowboy from Montana, and a simple tract. These were the instruments God used to lead Ruslan into what he often describes as the best decision he ever made.

Clay Bedford and Ruslan, Lutsk, Ukraine, 1994

CHAPTER 5

Is Anything Impossible with God?

Ruslan and I forged a special friendship during my month in Ukraine. He says that a week after meeting me, he was already thanking God that he'd met his future wife! Though I thought Ruslan was handsome and wonderful, I didn't think it was possible to know such things so quickly. Besides that, I was a student doing my DTS, and my focus wasn't supposed to be on romance, but on ministry!

When I think of my first two weeks in Ukraine, I can't deny that I was swept up in a beautiful love story. I fell in love with the Ukrainian people as our team ministered in hospitals, orphanages, and universities as well as through open-air evangelism on the streets. I also found myself falling for a Ukrainian guy who caused my heart to flutter every time he came near. He was so kind and caring, such a gentleman to everyone. He was easy to talk to, and our conversations often stretched late into the night.

One day, as we all walked through the town square, Ruslan disappeared around a corner. He reappeared with a red rose that he presented to me in front of my entire team. My face turned as red as the rose, and I endured constant teasing the rest of the day.

Two weeks into our outreach, our group of seventeen split into two teams. I was assigned to the team headed for Ukraine's Crimean Peninsula.

This meant I wouldn't be coming back to Lutsk, where Ruslan would continue to interpret for our team there.

Our departure for the twenty-six-hour train ride to Crimea felt like something out of a World War II movie. It rained as we hurried down the dimly lit streets of Lutsk, past darkened shops and green-domed Orthodox churches, to catch a 2:30 a.m. train.

As we stood on the station platform, Ruslan took my hand. "Please be careful and safe. I will be praying for you and the team." Then leaning over, he placed a gentle kiss on my forehead and drew me into his arms. "I will also be praying that God will show us where our special friendship might grow," he whispered into my ear.

Moments later, the last call sounded to get on the train. I jumped on, watching as Ruslan jogged alongside us waving goodbye. When I found my cabin room, one of the other students asked if I was okay. It was only then that I realized I had tears streaming down my face.

A year went by, with Ruslan and me writing letters to each other. We decided it was best to just be friends because the great distance between Idaho and Ukraine made a romantic relationship seem impossible. Mail took weeks to travel between us. Phone calls cost more than three dollars per minute. I was starting my freshman year at Seattle Pacific University, and Ruslan's life was six thousand miles away from mine. Yet as hard as I tried, I couldn't get him out of my mind.

Undeniably, those first four weeks of outreach in Ukraine had changed my life. I had not only fallen for Ruslan, but I had also fallen in love with the Ukrainian people, and my dream now was to equip myself for ministry and return to Ukraine as quickly as possible.

I probably would have stayed in Ukraine after my DTS outreach had it not been for a promise I made to my parents to get a college education. I think my father wanted assurances that I wouldn't pursue some wild idea about becoming a missionary after DTS. To him, going to university meant a degree, a career, and a responsible way of making money. I wasn't opposed to getting a university degree, I just missed Ukraine.

When I discovered that SPU had a Russian language program, I signed up for every class I could get. Russian grammar, Eastern European literature, the history of Russia. I wanted to learn all I could about Slavic culture.

I was overjoyed when I discovered that two of my dorm mates, Luba and Marina, were from Ukraine and Russia. They quickly became two of my closest friends.

The next summer, I was invited to return to Ukraine to serve for two weeks at a church where Ruslan worked. I couldn't say yes fast enough. I traveled there with a new friend, Michele Lind, who had been to Ukraine the previous year. I took this trip seriously. I knew that seeing Ruslan would stir up feelings again, but I promised the Lord that I would keep my focus on the ministry.

Upon our arrival in Kyiv, Ruslan and his pastor, Sasha, welcomed us warmly. They grabbed our luggage and headed to their car. As we arrived at the car, I halted in disbelief. It was the smallest Ford Fiesta I had ever seen. Where would we fit four people, two seventy-pound backpacks, and the guitar we had brought for the church? To my amazement, we did it. Michele and Pastor Sasha sat in the front seats, while Ruslan and I crammed into a small space in back. That meant very close proximity to Ruslan during the five-hour drive to Lutsk.

Lord, I can tell you right now, if this is a test, I am going to fail! And fail I did. For the next two weeks, although I was on a mission and serious about my ministry to the youth of Lutsk, I fell head over heels all over again for their youth pastor. I had never felt this way before. In the moments we found together just the two of us, I was dizzy, delirious, swept off my feet as if we were the only two people alive on Earth.

God, why is this happening? I asked in prayer one day, walking by myself along the shore of a small pond near Pastor Sasha's house. *I am about to completely lose my heart to this guy if I haven't already, but I just don't see how a future is possible for us. I don't think it's right to give him hope. I will leave for the US in just a few days, and I have no idea when or if I will ever see him again. God please, I want to do the right thing.*

I had convinced myself that a relationship was impossible. I needed to release Ruslan to his life, and me to mine. As I prayed for strength, I heard a whisper of a voice fill my mind, *Beloved, is anything impossible for me?*

Lord, is that you? Are you telling me there is a future for this relationship? There was no reply, but I felt the conviction of the Holy Spirit. I had not asked God if a relationship was possible. I had decided it wasn't, and I had asked for strength to resist my feelings. Now the Lord was reminding me that nothing was impossible with him.

There was no plan, no blueprint, no timeline, but on a walk the next day, Ruslan looked me in the eyes and told me he loved me. I couldn't help but respond, "I love you too."

When the day came for me to leave Ukraine again, we committed our relationship to God and asked him to lead us into whatever future he had for us. I didn't know how it could work, but I was ready to wait as long as it took. I had found the man I wanted to spend my life with. I just needed to get through three years of university first.

As I stepped onto the airport escalator that would take me to my gate, Ruslan stood at the bottom watching me go. I couldn't keep my tears from flowing. Michele had already gone up, and as I made my way toward our gate, I was crying so hard that I walked right past the customs agent who was checking passports. I wondered if he understood that I was leaving my heart in his country.

It was two years before Ruslan and I saw each other again—two very difficult years, not only for us, but also for the people of Ukraine. The whole country was struggling economically. Ruslan's mom earned just fifty dollars per month, and most days Ruslan and his family survived on root vegetables from their garden, buckwheat, or ramen noodles. It was during that painful time that I received this letter from Ruslan:

> Dear Sharyn,
>
> Though my feelings for you haven't changed, the situation in Ukraine is very difficult. I don't see any way I could provide a life for us here. You deserve more than what I can give you. I don't feel God is calling me to live in the United States. I am needed here, in my country, now more than ever.
>
> May God bless you, always.
>
> All my love,
>
> Ruslan

I was crushed. All I could do was place the love I had for Ruslan into God's hands and hope for another day, when circumstances might be different. A year went by, and I settled into my last year as a university student. That spring I was a bridesmaid three times, and I couldn't help but notice my own longing for marriage.

Lord, I'm not sure what I'm supposed to do with this desire for marriage I feel so strongly these days, especially since I still feel this call to missions in Ukraine.

One afternoon, I was chatting with my friend Evelyn about trying to reconcile my feelings about missions and marriage.

"Do you feel like God is saying you can't have both?" Evelyn asked.

"I don't know, but lately I've just been feeling like he's asking me to give my singleness to him. To stop worrying and wondering about the future in this area."

"Then I think that's exactly what you should do!" Evelyn said. "He holds your future, Sharyn. He will guide you perfectly."

When I entrusted to God my longing for marriage, a great peace and freedom followed.

I graduated from Seattle Pacific University in 2000, and instead of finding a "real job" as my father hoped, I signed up for a nine-month ministry apprenticeship in Simferopol, the political capital of Ukraine's Autonomous Republic of Crimea. The apprenticeship would give me the opportunity to minister among various people groups in Crimea. The previous summer, I had served at a local church that had an ongoing outreach to the Crimean Tatars, a Russian-speaking Muslim people group. My Russian was much improved, and I was looking forward to practicing it.

I was practicing trust in God too. While I was working in Simferopol, Ruslan contacted me, and we began writing again. It felt good to be in touch, and I hoped that we might see each other in the future.

In November, I took a week off to visit the youth group in Lutsk, where I had many friends. Ruslan lived in Lutsk, but as far as I knew, he would be out of town while I was there. He frequently traveled throughout the country interpreting for an American missionary. As my train came into Lutsk, I thought about that dark night several years ago when I said goodbye to Ruslan on this very platform. I was sad that I wouldn't see him on this trip. Wherever he was, I hoped he was doing well. I grabbed my bags, stepped off the train, and to my surprise, came face-to-face with Ruslan. I wasn't expecting him, but it felt so good to see him again. As silly as it might sound, I knew instantly that something was about to change. It was like this was a moment God had written from the beginning for our lives, and now we were finally stepping into it.

Ruslan took my bags and led me to the apartment where I was staying. In the days and weeks that followed, he made it clear that he was ready to pursue me, and marriage.

As Christmas approached, I was getting ready for a quick trip to the USA followed by a visit with Ruslan in Lutsk on my way back to Crimea. My problem was I had not yet told anyone back in the States that Ruslan and I were dating again. My mom and my closest friends knew what it had been like for me, believing for a future together and then having to let go of that dream. I wanted to be sure about the future of our relationship before I broke the news to everyone.

Now, as I called my mom that Sunday evening for our weekly ten-minute phone call, all that I was able to afford, I came right to the point.

"Mom, you aren't going to believe this, but Ruslan and I are seeing each other again. It's serious. He's looking for a ring. I know we've had our ups and downs over the years, so I'm asking God for his confirmation that he is calling us into marriage. What do you think?"

There was a brief silence on the line.

"Honey, I don't know why I never told you this. But three years ago, when Ruslan sent you the letter saying he didn't think a relationship was possible, he also sent me a letter. He asked for my forgiveness for the way he knew he was hurting you, and he tried to explain his reasons. I was so impressed that this young man from Ukraine would even think to consider my thoughts and feelings. I wrote him back. Honey, we've been writing to each other ever since. I pray for him almost every day. I know that God will lead you in just the right way, but I think Ruslan is a very, very special person."

I was shocked. Speechless. My mom was my closest confidant. How had she neglected to mention that the man I was considering marrying had been her pen pal for three years? Or that she had invested three years of prayer into his life? I couldn't believe it. If there was ever confirmation to be found, I was quite sure this was it.

Ruslan asked me to marry him over chicken noodle soup and pizza at a quaint little café just off the center square in Lutsk. Though he had planned a more romantic proposal, he had the ring in his pocket and couldn't wait to put it on my finger. I didn't mind one bit!

We married in the open air, on a sun-kissed fall afternoon near the shores of Priest Lake, Idaho, on September 8, 2001. We had written our own vows; I recited mine in Russian, and Ruslan recited his in English.

Truly nothing is impossible with God! Somehow the Lord saw fit to bring together a young girl from middle-of-nowhere northern Idaho with a young man from the former Soviet Union. Somehow this cross-cultural, transatlantic, long-distance relationship had defied all the odds. Geography, economics, callings—nothing we had thought were obstacles kept Ruslan and me apart in the end. God graciously gave each of us the one we loved and launched us together in the work of our dreams—serving the people of Ukraine.

Ruslan and Sharyn, our very first picture together
Lutsk, Ukraine, April 1996

Our wedding day, Priest Lake, Idaho, September 8, 2001

Sharyn and Ruslan with Loren Cunningham, founder of Youth With A Mission, at the Leadership Training School in Kyiv, September 2002

CHAPTER 6

YWAM Simferopol

During our first two years of marriage, Ruslan and I spent time in the USA, Ukraine, and Central Asia. Ruslan had never gone through a DTS, so we enrolled as a married couple with the lecture phase in Kyiv and our outreach in Kyrgyzstan. It was during our DTS that we were invited by Sasha and Nina Gurov to be part of a team starting a new YWAM base in Simferopol, Crimea.

In January 2003 we packed up our few belongings, including Ruslan's mountain bike and my guitar, and made the move to Simferopol. We had felt God's call to develop a branch of YWAM Family Ministries in Crimea, alongside a DTS program, over the next few years.

Simferopol was a great location for pioneering an international ministry. It was the hub of Crimea's regional government and industries and one of the most culturally diverse areas in Ukraine. Crimea was populated by not only Ukrainians and Russians but also people from Central Asia, Germany, Greece, and Armenia. Many other lesser-known people groups also made up its rich and varied ethnic identity.

Tourism was also a big industry, and the beautiful beach cities of Sudak, Alupka, Alushta, Yalta, and Yevpatoria drew people from all over the world. Relaxing on the Black Sea's picturesque beaches, exploring the many historical locations, and hiking in beautiful surroundings made this an area anyone would want to visit. But the people of Crimea also had a troubled side. Our hearts were burdened for this land that had some of the highest rates in Europe of alcoholism, drug addiction, HIV, divorce, institutionalized children, and corruption. Our little YWAM team longed to bring the light of God's love into those dark places.

Our main focus in developing YWAM Family Ministries in Crimea was to use a seminar called Blessing Generations in partnership with Family Foundations International. These seminars taught about the seven critical times in life that God intended us to receive blessing in order to establish identity and destiny for our lives as well as the truth that God wants to impart to each person at these critical times in our lives. The program presented excellent information on relationships, marriage, and parenting, but the real success was the inner healing and ministry that happened during the small-group sessions. Over the span of a decade, we organized more than fifty of these seminars and saw hundreds of people receive healing from past woundedness as well as recommit themselves to their marriages and families.

In the first years of our base's ministry, YWAM Simferopol also launched several Discipleship Training Schools, a successful preschool program, a thrift store, and a Christian bookstore. We partnered with local orphanages and churches and saw many wonderful ministries take place as DTS students and visiting teams came through our city and sowed into many towns and villages throughout the Crimean Peninsula. Many of our DTS students were coming to us from partnerships we had with church-led rehab centers, so our DTS program truly encompassed discipleship in every area of life.

We loved how our focus on family and relationships interconnected. Our preschool program was a great platform for offering parenting and marriage seminars. The thrift store connected with these young families as well, as they would come in search of toys and clothing for their families. And all these endeavors allowed us to get helpful and wholesome books for children and adults into many homes throughout Simferopol and beyond.

One of my favorite outreach locations was a halfway house for children in the town of Sholkino on the Azov Sea, a three-hour drive from Simferopol. We volunteered at this location every time YWAM Simferopol hosted a visiting outreach team. Of course, the children were the focus of our ministry, and they loved the games and gifts we brought with our Vacation Bible School–type programs. However, we also were very intentional about building relationships with the staff. Because this was a halfway house, a place where children stayed for only a few months until they could be placed in an orphanage or with a family, we saw a different set of children every time we visited. The staff, however, were the same. They told us time and time again how our visits brought them and the children so much life and light and how moved they were that we never forgot them even though they were in such a remote location. Over the years, we had many opportunities to share the love of Jesus with the wonderful women who worked at this location.

During our years in Simferopol, the Lord blessed us in so many ways. Our two beautiful baby girls were born, Gloria and Emily, exactly two years and two weeks apart. Ruslan's sister, Angela, and her daughter, Micaela, moved in with us. They had previously been living in Argentina, where Angela had immigrated years earlier. Our house was full of languages—English, Russian, Ukrainian, and Spanish! On one occasion, when Gloria was just two years old, she asked me, "Mommy, can I have some *soko, pozhalusta?*" I tried to speak only English with the girls, and Ruslan only Russian, so I responded to her mixed-up sentence this way: "Would you like some juice, Gloria?" Her reply? "*Sí,* Mama!" Oh, the poor girl! English, Spanish, and Russian all mixed together!

When Gloria was just six months old, we began to wonder what it would be like to purchase a house. Although we had no money to put toward such an endeavor, we felt that just as God was providing for a rent check every month, he could just as easily provide for a mortgage payment if that was his will. In prayer one afternoon, the day before Thanksgiving, we told the Lord we would do our part and investigate property options, educating ourselves on the housing market. Then we would trust that the Lord would provide the next steps if he so chose.

The next day our missionary community gathered for our traditional Thanksgiving celebration. As we were standing in line for the feast of turkey, pies, and mashed potatoes, Julie Morgenstern invited Ruslan and me to sit and eat with her and her husband, Mark.

The Morgensterns, together with their four boys, were some of the first missionaries from the United States to make Simferopol their home. I had been to their house many times for our women's Bible study group.

As we sat down to dinner, Julie mentioned that they were making plans to move back to the States. "Yesterday we were talking about putting our house on the market to sell, and you and Ruslan came to mind. We were wondering if you might be interested in buying our house."

Ruslan and I just stared at her, dumbstruck. Not even twenty-four hours earlier, we had given to the Lord this crazy idea about buying a house for our family. And on that very same day, Mark and Julie had been talking about offering to sell their home to us.

After touring the house, we felt a huge peace that God was leading us to purchase it. Although we didn't have a penny yet, we prayed about how much money we could offer the Morgensterns. One week later, we had an agreement. Mark and Julie gave us until the end of December to decide if we would be able to raise the funds, and then until May of the following year to pay them in full. On December 31, dear friends of ours, Kirk and Sally Scammell, felt a prompt from the Lord to loan us the funds to purchase the house. Four months after our humble prayer entrusting to God our desire to purchase a home, we moved into one. A year later, we received all the funds needed to pay back the loan in full. It was a miracle story, and one we love to tell!

Without fail, whether in our family life or in the ministry of YWAM Simferopol, God graciously kept teaching us that nothing is impossible for him.

CHAPTER 7

God's Mysterious Ways

As we moved into our eighth year of life and ministry in Simferopol, we found ourselves at somewhat of a crossroads. We had hoped that by now we'd have a large and well-established multicultural staff, but sadly, our team was down to just us and our base leaders, Sasha and Nina. Now Sasha and Nina were wondering if their season of serving with YWAM was ending. We began to question if it was time for us to move on too.

As we began to seek the Lord as to what the future might hold, we talked about the possibility of starting a YWAM base in another city, but Ruslan was reluctant. Although he was a capable leader, he preferred jobs that served and supported others and allowed him to stay in the background. After I brought it up again, he surprised me by responding, "If the national leader of YWAM Ukraine comes to my house and asks me to start another base here in Crimea, I'll pray about it. Otherwise, I don't think that is something I would want to do."

Well, that's that, I thought. Sasha Volyanyk, our national leader, lived on the opposite side of the country and hadn't been to Crimea in quite some time. As several more months went by, I decided that the Lord must not intend for us to pursue my idea. Then we received a surprise visit from Sasha.

Sasha asked to meet with us, and over breakfast at our favorite café, he explained that the decision had been made to close down YWAM Simferopol. Although it was sad to see our base close, at the same time it released us to pursue other possibilities.

Then, with a thoughtful look on his face, Sasha turned to Ruslan and asked, "Would you consider opening another YWAM base here in Crimea?"

Ruslan and I were both quiet. I could hear my heart beating and felt goose bumps moving up my arms.

With a grin, Ruslan looked Sasha in the eye and said, "I would be willing to pray about that."

We left the café filled with a sense of awe that the Lord had just started us down a new path. It was a holy moment, as all new beginnings are—one pregnant with possibilities we couldn't yet imagine.

We left for a furlough in the USA just a few weeks later and began to share with people there the possibility of starting a new YWAM base in Crimea. We talked with pastors, mentors, and old friends, and each one felt certain this change was of God. As we flew back to Ukraine in the spring of 2011, we were confident that God had confirmed his word to us, but the big question was, where should we launch this ministry center?

One location that kept coming up was the city of Sevastopol on the southwestern coast of Crimea. We had a connection with a church there that had been sending its members to YWAM schools since the mid-1990s. Theoretically speaking, we had a whole church of former YWAMers who likely would support a new base there.

Sevastopol had long been one of my favorite destinations on the Crimean Peninsula. Because of its strategic location on the Black Sea, it has a colorful history. It was occupied at various times by the Greeks, Romans, Byzantines, Mongols, Turks, and Russians. On the outskirts of Sevastopol is the ruins of Chersonesus, a Greek colony whose origins reach back to the first century, as well as the vast Inkerman cave monastery, both instrumental in spreading Christianity. Sevastopol is where the Charge of the Light Brigade took place, seared in public memory by Lord Tennyson's classic poem. More recently it was home base of the Soviet Union's famed Black Sea Fleet, and even after the fall of Communism in Moscow, Russia was allowed through a treaty with Ukraine to keep an active military base in Sevastopol.

One morning, after weeks of praying without any definitive direction, Ruslan offered a bold prayer. "Lord," he said, "would you confirm to us before the end of this day if we are to move to Sevastopol or not?"

Prayers like this used to scare me because I was concerned that God might not say anything. We didn't know it yet, but the Lord was teaching us to be bold in prayer, to take bigger steps of faith, and to grow in our trust and understanding of his workings in our lives.

That afternoon a repairman came over to install a hot water heater. We had hired this man before, but we didn't really know him. He and Ruslan chatted amicably during the installation. When Ruslan was getting ready to pay him, the man looked at him and said, "Why do you guys choose to live here in Simferopol? You should just go and do whatever you do in Sevastopol. It's a nicer place to live."

Ruslan looked at him, shocked. The guy had no idea that we were even thinking about moving—he certainly didn't know about Ruslan's prayer that morning about Sevastopol. We took this to be God's answer and began to seek his guidance more specifically for our next steps.

One Sunday we set out on a scouting venture. We were late as usual, speeding down the highway to get to the one o'clock service of God's Revival Church in Sevastopol. The girls were playing quietly in the backseat, and I was contemplating the significance of this little trip. Sevastopol was about a two-hour drive from Simferopol, and we hadn't visited this church in five years, even though it was full of good friends and ministry acquaintances. Since no one knew we were coming, our plan was to slip into the back row and casually say hello after the service.

About halfway there, Ruslan glanced over toward me and said something completely unexpected. "Sharyn, if it's God's will that we open a YWAM base in Sevastopol, then let it be that the pastor not only remembers us this morning, but that he invites us to move there and work in his church."

I know that with God all things are possible, but I thought the chances of that happening were about as great as me making sense of the Russian grammar system—not likely! We hadn't talked to the pastor in several years.

I whispered an apprehensive, "Okay," and resigned myself to see what God's reaction might be to my husband's "fleece," a rare biblical approach to guidance used by Gideon in Judges 6.

We were late in getting to Sevastopol, but we finally made it to the service at God's Revival Church. After finding a parking place, we snuck into the back of the church during a worship song. Because of our untimely arrival, I hoped we wouldn't be noticed.

When the singing concluded, Pastor Yuri Rudenko took to the podium to welcome the church body and make a few announcements. As he did so, he looked out over the auditorium and suddenly paused mid-sentence, staring straight at our family. "Wow, look who's here!" he exclaimed. "It's the Borodin family! Welcome. We are so glad to see you! Wouldn't it be amazing if we could convince these guys to move to Sevastopol and be part of our church service every Sunday?"

With that Pastor Yuri went on with his greetings and then shared the message he had prepared for that morning.

He had said exactly what Ruslan had put out as a fleece before the Lord—that the pastor would remember us and invite us to move to Sevastopol and work in his church. I gave my husband a sly look. "Well, it looks like he remembered us!" I whispered.

After the service, Pastor Yuri stopped to talk with us and, as if he had been eavesdropping on our conversations over the past few weeks, straight up asked us if we had ever considered opening a YWAM base in Sevastopol.

Ruslan smiled and answered, "Actually, that is something we have been praying about. We were wondering what you might think about that?"

We began to talk about a partnership between Pastor Yuri's church and a new YWAM base. We left Sevastopol that day feeling certain that this was where God was leading us. In the weeks and months that followed, word began to get out about our plans, and we received messages from friends and colleagues who were interested in working with us there.

We received so much confirmation that at one point I remember telling God that I didn't need any more—we had gotten the message! Everywhere we went, it felt like the Lord was confirming we were on the right path.

Our family was excited for our new direction but still had important work to do in Simferopol, followed by a year in leadership training, before we anticipated launching a new YWAM base in Sevastopol. As we continued our work in the city that had been our home for almost ten years, we would never have guessed that in less than a year's time neighborhoods we walked through every day would be broadcast worldwide as breaking news. We were about to find ourselves at ground zero of an event that would change our lives and the lives of all Ukrainians forever. The Crimea we knew and loved was about to vanish.

The Borodin family: Gloria, Ruslan, Sharyn, and Emily, 2009

YWAM Simferopol's family store stocked clothing, toys, and handmade baby blankets donated from throughout the USA and was the only Christian bookstore in our city

Ruslan, Sharyn, Gloria, Ruslan's sister Angela, her daughter Micaela, and Emily
Simferopol, Ukraine, 2013

CHAPTER 8

Ice, Fire, and Faithfulness

In March 2013 I traveled to Budapest, Hungary, for our annual YWAM Family Ministries Forum. On a hotel boat secured along the banks of the Danube River, YWAM workers from all over Europe gathered for fellowship and training to advance our common calling to build up strong Christ-centered families among the nations. With close to 150 full-time staff, YWAM Family Ministries is active in about twenty European nations. Throughout the year family-ministry staff run family camps, Family DTS, marriage courses, and family-ministry schools, just to name a few of the ways they serve.

For this trip, our daughter Gloria, age six, was my traveling companion. When we reached the airport for the journey home, we were told there would be no traveling that day due to an uncharacteristically late winter storm in Kyiv. The city had received more than three feet of snow in twenty-four hours. The next day, we managed to find a flight to Kyiv, where we ran into our next problem: how to get the rest of the way home. Train travel throughout Ukraine was at a standstill.

The train ride from Kyiv to Simferopol was sixteen hours long, and we were in a hurry. In just a week's time, a team from Idaho would arrive—high school students on their spring-break mission trip. There was so much to do before their arrival. I needed to get back to Ruslan and Emily so that Ruslan could go to Kyiv to meet the team at Boryspil International Airport.

Along with thousands of others, Gloria and I needed to find a way home and rebook our tickets. As we walked into the enormous Grand Central station, I couldn't believe the number of people. I tightened my hold on Gloria's hand as we made our way to the ticket booths. The train we needed didn't depart for another four hours, so I felt confident we could reach the ticket counter before then.

However, as we entered the ticket-booth area, I stared in disbelief. I counted eight lines of about fifty people each, everyone waiting for their turn to get a refund, to purchase new tickets, or both. Gloria and I picked the line that looked the shortest.

An hour passed. I made a little chair out of our luggage for Gloria to sit on and pulled out some activity books to entertain her. Another hour went by. After three hours in line, we had witnessed several unpleasant shouting matches over how slowly the lines were moving. I began to doubt that we would make our train.

With only an hour left until our departure, there were still more than twenty people in front of us. My mind was working on backup plans. *Where would we spend the night? Could we get another train? How could I prepare for the team that was coming?* Finally, with just forty-five minutes to spare, I looked at Gloria and did what I should have done hours earlier.

"Gloria," I said, "I'm concerned we are not going to be able to get our tickets in time to catch our train today. Let's pray together and ask Jesus for help." I knelt beside her, and I simply prayed, "Jesus, we want to get home. Would you please provide a way for us to get our train tickets in time for us to leave today? In Jesus' name, amen."

Gloria said amen too and then went back to her workbook, while I went back to counting how many people were in front of us.

About ten minutes after our prayer, a woman approached me and said hello. "I have been watching you and your daughter for the past couple of hours," she explained. "I took it upon myself to save you a spot in that line over there, and your turn is coming up next."

The woman urged us to grab our things and follow her. Before I even knew what was happening, I was in front of the ticket window, and the clerk was asking me where we were headed.

"Ah, I need two tickets to Simferopol please," I stammered.

"Names."

"Sharyn Borodina and Gloria Borodina."

"That will be 280 hryvnia."

"Here it is," I replied.

"Your train leaves in thirty minutes. Next!"

I grabbed the tickets, Gloria's hand, and our suitcases and stepped out of the line feeling dazed. After three and a half hours of waiting, it had taken just five minutes to purchase our tickets. I looked around to find the woman who had helped us and couldn't see where she had gone. I felt like we had cut the line, but the people behind us had let us in as if that had been our spot all along.

Finally, I looked at my bright-eyed daughter and said, "Gloria, I think we have just experienced a miracle. I don't know why that woman helped us."

"Maybe she was an angel, Mommy?" Gloria said with a note of awe in her voice.

"Gloria, the Bible says that Jesus is our ever-present help in times of trouble. All we had to do was ask, and he provided for us. Let's always remember this day, okay?"

We took a moment to thank Jesus. Then we grabbed a pizza from the kiosk and made our way toward our train. To this day, Gloria remembers how Jesus answered our prayers and made a way for us to get home.

One week later, with great expectation, I was at the Simferopol train station waiting on the platform with Gloria, Emily, and their cousin Micaela for the arrival of Ruslan and the team from Idaho.

The group of seventeen juniors, seniors, college interns, and teachers was visiting us from House of the Lord Christian Church in Oldtown, Idaho. I had a special connection with their church. I occasionally attended youth group there during my high school years, and when I ventured out in missions, the church supported my endeavors.

The church operates a PK–12 Christian school that is a huge blessing in their community. When our girls reached school age, we asked the school board to allow them to be part of their educational system. The girls would be enrolled in the school whenever we were in Idaho. When we were in Ukraine, we would homeschool using the same curriculum.

The school is committed not only to providing an excellent education for their students but also to seeing students grow in their relationships with Jesus. To this end, the school takes juniors and seniors on a mission trip once every two years. It's an excellent opportunity for these kids to experience another culture far from home and to learn to trust Jesus at a deeper level. Ruslan and I had been talking with the principal for years about hosting one of these teams in Crimea.

The Idaho team had flown into Kyiv the day before and had spent sixteen hours on the train crossing the country to where the girls and I waited. I was overjoyed to see all their faces as they stepped off the train. They were exhausted after forty-eight hours of travel but ready to engage and be a blessing to our community.

We collected luggage and then piled into the bus that would take us on the three-hour ride to a little coastal village just outside Sevastopol, where the team would stay. The first part of their outreach would start the next day. As we drove through the countryside, I smiled as I watched our young guests' expressions. I knew exactly what they were thinking. There is something incredible about leaving home for the first time and entering a land where everything is different—roads, traffic systems, architecture, faces, food, even the interior of the bus. I couldn't wait to see what God would do in these teenagers.

For the next three days we would be staying at a new hotel owned by a member of our church there. We were some of the hotel's very first guests. The staff had a lovely lunch laid out for our arrival, and afterward we showed our visitors to their rooms so they could rest. The plan was to meet up in two hours for a walk down to the beach and a discussion about the weekend itinerary.

When everyone was settled in, I made my way to my own room on the second floor. The room was a little chilly, so I grabbed the remote to turn on the heating unit.

Nothing happened. The heater wouldn't turn on.

I checked to make sure everything was plugged in correctly, and that was when I smelled the first faint waft of smoke. *What?* I looked through the window and noticed fumes coming out of the exterior side of the unit. I stepped out of the room into the open-air hallway to see what was going on, and flames and black smoke suddenly shot out from the top of the heating unit—and from the hotel roof.

Without thinking, I yelled, "FIRE!" in English and then yelled it again in Russian. In the few seconds it took me to issue the alarm, the fire spread into the rafters. As flames and smoke billowed, I shouted for everyone to evacuate to the parking lot. Then, with a start, I realized I didn't know where my girls were. I had left them to finish their lunch while I helped the team find their rooms. Frantically, I ran down to the courtyard and saw my daughters and my niece standing there with wide eyes and quivering lips, watching as the hotel roof burst into flames.

I did a quick head count and sighed in relief that our whole group was present. As Ruslan and the hotel owner ran around doing whatever they could to contain the fire, I heard the sirens of an approaching fire truck.

Standing there with the others, I could barely move. I wanted to break down and cry. How could this be happening? We had just arrived. I feared we had done something to burn down this man's new hotel.

I looked around at the exhausted and terrified faces of our young visitors and just couldn't fathom how this could happen on the first day of their mission trip. As the fire grew in intensity, the realization hit me that I couldn't afford to lose control of my emotions, not when all these people were depending on me. Many on this team were the children of friends back in the States. Those friends had trusted me to take care of their kids. I took a deep breath and thought, *Okay, Sharyn. Pull it together. You need to look ahead and help this team move past this.*

I began by asking the team to gather their things and follow me to the end of the road, where we could regroup at a small café. As we walked to the café, I called our good friend Sergei, who was helping to host our team in Sevastopol. He had left us only about thirty minutes before, and we weren't planning to see him again until the next morning.

"Sergei," I said, "I don't know how exactly to put this, but the hotel caught fire. It's bad. And as crazy as that is for you to try and process at this moment, I need you to find another place we can stay and transportation for this team to get there—and quick!"

I was relieved to hear Sergei's calm response. He assured me of his help and said he was already on his way back to the hotel. Once off the phone, I sent up a quick prayer that Ruslan would be wise and safe as he did whatever he could to help put out the fire.

When we reached the café, I was informed that three of the boys on our team hadn't been able to grab any of their belongings on their way out the door. I realized this most likely meant that their passports, Bibles, computers, clothes, and other possessions had literally gone up in smoke. It was a surreal moment, but I could feel something in me—a strengthening voice leading me to look past the flames, the questions, and the uncertainties and to comfort this team.

"Guys, can I have your attention for a moment? I realize that this is a scary experience and not in any way how we planned to start off your time here." I made eye contact with each person, one by one. "I want you to know that you are going to be okay. We are going to find another hotel to stay in, you will get some rest, and we will not allow the enemy to steal from us the incredible plans God has for this outreach. What was lost in those flames are all things that can be replaced. Let's take a minute to give thanks for our safety and ask the Lord to help those trying to put out this fire. Let's pray for his peace as we move past this crisis."

As it turned out, the fire was due to an electrical problem—very likely the result of a rushed construction project. For the rest of that day and through the night, I spent hours talking on the phone with the pastor of the church, messaging with parents, speaking with the leaders of the team, and calling the American consulate to find out how to replace the passports. I marveled at how quickly the team, my girls, Ruslan, and I all bonded during those first twelve hours. Thankfully, the consulate in Kyiv issued temporary passports for the boys who had lost theirs in the fire, and the church in Idaho sent extra funds to help replace things that had been lost.

In the days that followed, the big joke was how the team had prayed in advance that God would light hearts on fire with the gospel message. They joked that maybe they should have been more specific when praying for fire. The enemy had tried to end the outreach before it started, but the result was one of the most anointed and fruitful outreaches we have ever hosted. The team led youth outreach in local villages, taught in our preschool program, visited local nursing homes, and spread the love of Jesus in impactful ways during their week in Crimea. God taught all of us to trust him and lean into each other like never before. The flames didn't define the story. The crisis and loss weren't the headline; the way we overcame it was. Little did we know that geopolitical coals were also smoldering throughout Eastern Europe and that the political friction sparking over Kyiv was about to erupt in flames.

House of the Lord Christian Academy outreach, ministering at our Smile preschool program, Sevastopol, Ukraine, spring 2013

The hotel fire! Spring 2013, near Sevastopol, Ukraine

Emily and Gloria holding American and Ukrainian flags at our church in Sevastopol, 2013

Emily (1st grade) and Gloria (3rd grade), House of the Lord Christian Academy, 2013

CHAPTER 9

The Maidan Revolution

I loved Ukraine. There was no place else I wanted to be. Yet living in this country had taught me how fortunate and blessed I was to have grown up in the United States. I wasn't in Ukraine long before I no longer took for granted things like hot water, good highways, public bathrooms, competent drivers, friendly police, good health care, and a political system that wasn't bought and paid for by corruption.

There has been so much corruption in Ukraine that I think the population by and large, especially on the everyday levels of society, just sees it as business as usual. So whether it is "gifting" your teacher a little something in return for an A on an exam, paying the "unofficial" price for getting the good medication at the hospital, paying off officials to expedite the opening of a business, or paying a police officer directly for a traffic citation, corruption has been present almost everywhere, keeping Ukraine from growing into the prosperous country it could be.

Ukraine has a highly educated, hard-working, and innovative population. It is a country rich in natural resources, and it is positioned perfectly to be an economic and cultural bridge between the West and East. But it has been hindered by an abusive system left behind after the fall of the

Soviet Union. I believe a new generation of Ukrainian leaders want to see this corrupt legacy ended, but such changes take time.

In November 2013, Ukraine's president Victor Yanukovych was talking with leaders from the West about free-trade agreements with the European Union. Earlier that year, Ukraine's parliament voted overwhelmingly for a new agreement with the EU. Closer economic ties with the West would have boosted the country's commerce, but the prospect of such agreements drew immediate opposition from Russia.

Yanukovych yielded to Russian pressure and pulled out of the trade agreement. His move for closer ties with Russia sparked immediate protests in Kyiv's Maidan Square and across the nation. This resistance to Russian tyranny became known as the Maidan Revolution.

We were in Idaho when this mass protest began. By the time we returned to Crimea in January 2014, the protests were spreading across the nation. Our conundrum was that while our friends and colleagues in western Ukraine were experiencing an unprecedented revolution, it seemed like business as usual in Simferopol. The reason for this is that Crimea is a very pro-Russia part of Ukraine. After World War II, Soviet dictator Joseph Stalin forcibly deported 230,000 of the native Crimean Tatar people to Uzbekistan in Central Asia. Once the Tatars were gone, Stalin relocated Russian families from throughout the Soviet Union who moved right into the empty homes of the Tatars, taking ownership of not only the house but everything left behind. As a result, the Crimean Peninsula's dominant population became Russian.

Despite the unrest across Ukraine, we were happy to return from our furlough in the States to our neighborhood on Barisheva Street in Simferopol. Our preschool program was flourishing, our little family thrift store was running smoothly, and we were so excited about our plans for the year. In about a month, we would leave these ministries in the capable hands of our onsite team and move to Ternopil in western Ukraine for one year of training under the YWAM national director. Then we would move to Sevastopol and begin pioneering a YWAM base there.

On February 18, protests in Kyiv took a bloody turn, as government forces fired on peaceful protesters. We called Yuri and Tanya Sokolovski, our YWAM Ukraine Family Ministry leaders, as they joined thousands of other Ukrainians on Independence Square. We could hear shooting and yelling in the background. I'll never forget what it felt like as Yuri said, "If we don't see you again, we'll see you in heaven." Then the line went dead.

Though Yuri and Tanya survived, hundreds were injured or killed when Yanukovych's men shot into the crowds. Opposition forces responded by taking over police stations and government offices in the cities of Lviv, Ivano-Frankivsk, Uzhhorod, and Ternopil. The whole world was now watching and wondering what Vladimir Putin's response would be. At the time, however, the leader of the Russian Federation had his hands full hosting the Winter Olympics in Sochi. With so much world attention focused on him, it seemed unlikely there would be a significant response before the closing ceremony on February 23.

By this point, many of our colleagues who worked with other mission organizations were being called out of Crimea. It was puzzling to us because it was still peaceful in Crimea. There were no protests and no threats of any sort coming from Russia. What did these other organizations know that we didn't? There was no evidence suggesting an invasion of Crimea, and yet we were living daily with a terrible feeling of dread.

As the 2014 Winter Olympics in Russia ended, Ukraine's opposition formed an interim government. The parliament granted full amnesty to protesters, and Yanukovych escaped by helicopter to Russia. The new government charged him with the murders of one hundred Maidan protesters. In just a few days, he went from president to enemy of the state.

When the newly instated Ukrainian authorities raided his palace, they found astonishing opulence. Nearly every interior surface was stamped with gilding and polished marble. The estate boasted a pier for his yacht, an equestrian club, tennis courts, hunting grounds, a museum for his exotic cars, a golf course, an ostrich farm, a dog kennel, and numerous fountains. In a country where the average Ukrainian earned less than four thousand dollars annually, such luxury was shocking. It was now exposed in Ukraine's news media.

As this news unfolded in western Ukraine, we couldn't shake the feeling that something bad was about to happen, though we hoped and prayed it wouldn't.

On the morning of February 27, I awoke from a fitful sleep and passed by the girls' bedroom. Now ages six and eight, they slept without a care in the world. I wished I felt such peace. As I walked down to the kitchen to get a cup of coffee, I discovered that Ruslan had been up since before dawn. He had been following the news, reading his Bible, and praying that God would give us wisdom. I took one look at my husband's worried face and forgot all about my coffee.

"Sharyn," Ruslan said with a calm but serious demeanor, "the local news stations are reporting that, during the night, unmarked, masked special forces took control of government buildings in Crimea. At this point, military invasion of Ukraine is a certainty, and the fact is it's probably already started."

As I tried to process what my husband was saying, I didn't understand what it meant that these special forces were unmarked. I asked him to explain.

"It means that they are trying to keep the government that they are affiliated with a secret. Of course, these soldiers are from Russia. Everyone knows this, but Russia will want plausible deniability that they are backing this takeover. Whatever happens next will not be good for Crimea or for Ukraine."

There was a pause and then the words I dreaded hearing. "It's time for you and the girls to go."

I can't tell you how agonizing it had been over the past weeks to try to decide whether to stay or to go. Ruslan and I wouldn't have entertained the idea of leaving if not for our children. The reason was simple—Crimea was our home. It was also home to the precious people who formed our community. How could we leave? How could we desert the place and people we loved so much in what might be their greatest moments of need?

No matter how much we talked and prayed, I hadn't been able to accept the idea of leaving. Uncharacteristically, my decision-making ability seemed to freeze in this situation. So instead of trying to figure everything out, I had decided to trust the Lord to lead my husband to make the right decision for our family. If we needed to flee, God would show Ruslan, and we would do whatever he thought was best.

Now that the moment had arrived, Ruslan didn't hesitate. His priority was to get his family to a safe place. He would stay and weather whatever came, but we would be on the next train out—period.

Putting our evacuation plan into action was one of the saddest moments of my life. But it was also a relief. Now I wondered what we would tell our girls. How could we explain to them that a military invasion was in progress and that we were just hours away from seeing tanks and other armored vehicles in the streets? How would we tell them that the only home they had ever known might be enveloped by armed conflict? And that amid these potential situations, their papa was going to stay behind to help as needed? It was terrifying.

I hate the word *evacuating*. It feels so final, so hopeless, and yet we were doing it. We were leaving because we didn't know what tomorrow would bring, but we guessed it wouldn't be anything good. If this was our last day living in Crimea, we didn't want Gloria and Emily to remember it as the day World War III broke out in our backyard.

There was no need to wake the girls quite yet. I grabbed the phone and started making calls to our remaining expat community. The news hadn't yet hit Western media outlets, so our English-speaking community wasn't aware of what was happening. For many, our call set their own evacuation plans in motion.

I grabbed one small suitcase, threw in a week's worth of clothes, and added the girls' schoolbooks and my journals.

When we woke the girls, we explained a version of the situation that was truthful but left out all the scary details. As those precious faces looked at us with groggy eyes, we told them that they would be taking the train to Ternopil with me and Auntie Shannon, a close friend and fellow missionary, and that Ruslan and our dog, Mimi, would meet us there. I explained, "We are going early to look for the house where we will live during our year in Ternopil. When we find it, we will make it pretty, so it will be a surprise for Papa and Mimi when they join us next week."

As I hurriedly prepared breakfast, my mind began to wander. *What if this is the last time I prepare a meal in this house? What if our departure is our last memory together in this place? What if this is the last time I see my husband?*

Other thoughts like these surfaced, but I blocked them out. I told myself, *Sharyn, you are just overdramatizing the situation.* Ever the optimist, I firmly told myself to visualize a better scenario and then focus on getting through the next twenty-four hours. The crisis fully engaged my coping mechanisms. I focused on simply taking the next step, while breathing prayers and trying to reassure myself that this crisis would have a happy ending for us.

That morning as Ruslan and his sister, Angela, loaded us onto the train, I realized how significant this moment was. I felt like a wartime wife saying goodbye to her husband who was about to be deployed to the front, yet for the sake of our girls I couldn't let myself realize those feelings of panic and fear. We all hugged and kissed each other and promised to meet soon in Ternopil. Then the girls positioned themselves by the window for the traditional goodbye.

On those rare occasions that we weren't traveling together, whichever one of us was staying home would always make sure we found the window of the other's cabin, blowing kisses, as we waited for the train to depart. The girls loved this tradition. As our train pulled out of Simferopol, they sat on the little table in front of the window and waved at their papa on the platform. They blew him kisses and made funny faces. In turn, Ruslan made silly faces at them and walked alongside the train as long as he could.

I'll never forget watching this endearing picture and wondering if Gloria and Emily would ever see their father again. Then I scolded myself for even thinking such a thing. Of course we would see each other again. This was just a hard goodbye. A goodbye taking us into unknown territory where anything could happen. Anything. We were about to learn, as Corrie ten Boom, author of *The Hiding Place*, so beautifully expressed, "You'll never know that Christ is all you need, until Christ is all you have."

Emily looking out the train window at Ruslan as our train prepared to leave Simferopol. Our train was the last to leave with the Ukrainian flag still flying. February 2014.

CHAPTER 10

A Safe Haven in Ternopil

Twenty-four hours later, on the other side of the country, we pulled into the train station in Ternopil. We were met by YWAM missionaries Andriy Futorsky and Sasha Volyanyk, who promptly delivered us to the YWAM building on Nova Street. As we shared our story, everyone said the same thing: There was no way Crimea would remain under Russian control. It was just a political move. Crimea was Ukrainian territory, everyone knew that. It would just take some time for things to get worked out. I felt less certain.

We soon learned that our train had been the last to cross the border under Ukrainian control. The airport had been shut down, and all the border crossings in Crimea were now controlled by Russian special forces. We heard terrifying stories from colleagues who had tried to leave the peninsula by car. The Russians pointed automatic weapons at them while accusing them of trying to smuggle valuables over the border.

Crimea now was making global headlines. Friends from around the world messaged us to see if we were okay. The invasion had taken everyone by surprise, and even the American embassy in Kyiv called us to get an update on what we were experiencing in Crimea.

Every major news agency on the planet was beelining toward Crimea. Several reporters interviewed Ruslan as he walked the streets of Simferopol. And it was a big story! Russia, pretending not to be Russia, had seized sovereign Ukrainian territory. Now it was trying to sell the fairytale that it was an inside job initiated by the Crimean local government. But the Russian flag was now flying in the town square, and soldiers dressed in camo, body armor, and face masks stood ready for attack.

I studied a photo Ruslan took of a soldier standing guard near the center square. The man's eyes were the only part of his face I could see, and they somehow touched my heart. This was someone's son. Someone's brother. What was his story? Did he even know why he was there? Did he care?

Day and night, I was talking on the phone and answering emails, giving others updates and direction for how to pray. I asked for prayer for Ruslan, for our ministries in Crimea, and for the whole political situation. I assured family and friends that the girls and I were safe in western Ukraine. I also checked in with our Crimean friends and colleagues, now scattered all over Ukraine, offering assistance. I scoured every news report I could find to see how the world was responding to this crisis.

Ruslan was getting our affairs in order as best he could and preparing to leave with our dog, Mimi, to join us in Ternopil. In the meantime, the girls and I began to look for a place to rent. When we heard about a townhouse just a fifteen-minute walk from the YWAM base, we jumped on it. I had decided that I would say yes to just about anything that was affordable and warm if it had a bathtub, a washing machine, and a place for our dog. We weren't going to be in Ternopil for more than a year, and we could make do with just about anything for that long.

The townhouse was indeed cheap and close to the YWAM base, but its other amenities left much to be desired. Even so, I felt peace about saying yes. I could live with a kitchen the size of a closet and an even smaller bathroom since it would just be for a year.

Upon signing the lease, the girls and I moved in, which didn't take long since we had only one suitcase. One perk about living in Ternopil was that the city had a secondhand store on every corner. Those shops enabled us to purchase bedding, curtains, decorations, and pots and pans. We also bought cold-weather shoes and clothes to enhance our limited wardrobe.

Our YWAM community blessed us with other needed supplies, and we tried to make things look cheerful and homey as we waited for Ruslan to join us.

A week later, he and Mimi arrived at the Ternopil train station. When we got to our townhouse and began carrying in our belongings, several of our neighbors came out to introduce themselves. Alla, a beautiful woman about my age, exclaimed, “I saw you and your daughters at one of the thrift shops. I am so excited that we are going to be neighbors!” She, her husband, Vadim, and their two daughters, Alina and Yana, lived together with her parents, Gregory and Galina, in the place next to ours.

We soon discovered they were also believers, and when they heard our story, they showered us with kindness. They gave us fresh eggs and canned preserves, had us over for meals, took us to their church, and showed us all the best shopping spots in town. They quickly became our close friends. I could see God’s hand connecting us to his people, and I felt more peace about the house that would be our home for the next year.

With Ruslan’s arrival in Ternopil, we tried to figure out what the next year would be like. Our original purpose for coming here was to train with the leadership for opening a new base in Crimea. Now it seemed prudent to push the pause button on those ambitions. Lance and Megan Roberts, who had just taken over leadership of YWAM Ternopil, jokingly said we had come as base leaders in training but now were “base leaders in waiting.” All of Ukraine was waiting to see what would happen next. In the meantime, we served various ministries at the base, found a ballet class and knitting club for the girls, and began to attend Calvary Chapel, which had a service in both English and Ukrainian.

As we began to engage with the Ternopil community, I discovered something that surprised me. Although I was thankful for our neighbors and YWAM colleagues, I didn’t feel much motivation to make friends. I didn’t want to put down roots here. I didn’t want this place to feel like our new home, even if just for a while. I was so afraid that we wouldn’t be able to go home to Crimea. I felt that liking anywhere else would be a betrayal of our vision. I told anyone who inquired that we were here just temporarily.

My problem was that it was easy to like Ternopil. We were shown kindness by even complete strangers. The YWAM community not only opened their homes and hearts to us, but they also loved and pursued our children. Valya from Russia, Yana from Kazakhstan, and so many others surrounded us with care and attention. This community of friendships sprouted up around us, and we leaned into it with grateful hearts. We had been warned by friends in Crimea that we would face discrimination in western Ukraine and were told not to speak Russian in this Ukrainian-speaking part of the country. Our experience, however, was the exact opposite. Everywhere we went, people showed us compassion and kindness. Since I didn't speak Ukrainian, and most of the population didn't speak English, Russian was the only language I could use to communicate with people. They often responded in Ukrainian, which was fine, even though I understood little of what they said. Often they would switch to Russian, knowing that we could communicate more effectively that way.

We were sad to learn that Ruslan's sister, Angela, and her daughter, Micaela, were leaving Crimea to move back to Argentina. They had lived with us for the past seven years and were like a second mother and sister to our girls. Saying goodbye to them brought home the reality to all of us, especially our children, that our departure from Crimea was based on serious circumstances. Even though we believed we would return, the occupation of Crimea was already bringing irrevocable change to our lives.

For months after Angela and Micaela left, Emily would cry and ask why they had to go. Our normally energetic and independent six-year-old was suddenly clingy and afraid to be left alone. Gloria, on the other hand, was angry. Being a mature eight-year-old, she understood that we had left Crimea for reasons other than what she had been told.

"Mom," she demanded, "why didn't you tell us the truth when we were still in Simferopol? You lied to us. How could you do that? I had a right to know what was really happening!"

"Honey, I am so sorry. We didn't know what to say. We didn't know exactly what was going to happen. We didn't want you to be scared, especially because Papa wasn't coming with us right away."

"I'm not a baby, Mom. I could have handled the truth. We may never get to go home again, and I didn't even get to say goodbye."

"Gloria, I haven't given up on going home, we just don't know when it will happen. Please forgive us for not knowing how to communicate to you the reality of the situation. I know it's hard to understand, but we were trying to do the best thing."

"I know, Mom. But it hurts my feelings that you didn't trust me. I still feel really mad."

Gloria's words hurt, but she was understandably upset at how we had handled things. I hoped that with God's help we could regain her trust. She wanted to know what was happening in Crimea because it was her home too.

As we processed the impact of being among the first displaced people out of Crimea, we realized how much was changing, and we felt the loss profoundly. Slowly, the shock of what had happened to us eased, and we settled into a new routine, in this temporary home, waiting to see what tomorrow would bring for our lives in Crimea.

On March 16, 2014, Russia held a highly publicized referendum to ostensibly allow the citizens of Crimea to choose their government. There were just two choices on the ballot: to join the Russian Federation or to become a self-governing territory. News agencies reported that more than 95 percent of voters cast their ballots to join the Russian Federation. I found it disheartening that they did not mention how few Crimeans actually voted, especially among the Crimean Tatar population. Many Crimeans felt there was no point in voting because the option to remain part of Ukraine was not on the ballot. Those who did vote experienced the sobering presence of armed men at the polling stations. Many world leaders condemned the election and Russia's actions, but the takeover was now in full swing. Crimea went from being "occupied" to being "annexed."

In April the situation went from bad to worse when fighting broke out in the Donbas region. Once again, Russian troops posing as locals were trying to take over an area where millions of Ukrainians lived. Putin announced that it was the right of this Russian-speaking part of Ukraine to choose their own destiny and to be annexed by Russia if that is what they desired.

By this time, the new government in Kyiv had organized itself well enough to mobilize the Ukrainian armed forces, which meant the unthinkable was now a reality—war in Ukraine. While Ukraine was fighting for its territorial integrity, Russia was doing everything it could to destabilize the country. In the months that followed, hundreds of thousands of Ukrainians were displaced from their homes, and there were thousands of casualties, both civilian and military. The country was in shock. And our way home was looking bleaker by the minute.

Unmarked special-forces soldiers in defensive positions surrounding the government buildings in the center of Simferopol, February 2014

Our first picture in front of the YWAM Ternopil base, Ternopil, Ukraine, 2014

CHAPTER 11

The Really Not-So-Good Year

As we began to settle into life in Ternopil, the climate was one of the big adjustments for us. Where Crimea was sunny and warm most of the year, we spent a month in Ternopil before the sun came out a single time. We realized what a gift the warm weather of Crimea was and felt the loss of it. Our immune systems also didn't transition well to the new climate or to the loads of stress we were enduring. That spring we had one bug after another as well as a bout of lice that we picked up from a team returning from outreach.

We had looked forward to summer, and in early July we had an opportunity to travel to YWAM Kyiv to join a gathering of our Ukraine Family Ministry team. We were so excited for this fun break with good friends at this YWAM campus near the beautiful Dnieper River.

Much to our dismay, our first morning there, the girls and I woke up with high fevers and blisters on our hands, feet, and mouth. On top of that, we discovered that we hadn't been successful in our attempts to get rid of the dreaded lice nits in our hair. A quick trip to the clinic diagnosed us with hand, foot, and mouth disease, a virus quite common in younger children, but rarely found in adults. We spent our entire week with YWAM Kyiv quarantined in our rooms.

On July 17, news broke that Russian-backed troops in the Donbas area had shot down Malaysian Airlines Flight 17, killing 298 passengers and crew, including 80 children. While the more than 160 commercial airliners that flew over eastern Ukraine that day stayed above an altitude of thirty-two thousand feet—thought to be high enough to avoid any danger from the conflict below—flight MH17 was shot down by a Buk missile, which can reach a height of eighty thousand feet. The missile was fired from rebel-held territory, and it is presumed that the plane was mistakenly thought to be Ukrainian military aircraft. We were heartbroken at such a needless loss of life and felt sure that the world would finally hold Russia accountable.

In early August, still recovering from all the bouts of illness over the past months, we decided to take some vacation time in the Carpathian Mountains. We were sorely in need of some fun, as the past five months had been anything but. We decided to splurge on a nice hotel with an outside swimming pool, and the girls were excited about this little adventure together.

The day of our departure, I woke up with a sharp pain in my gut. I thought it was just another phase of the virus I had been trying to get rid of since July. To be safe, we decided that we would stop at a private clinic in Lviv en route to our vacation destination so that I could get checked out. We hoped the clinic might have some medication that would help me feel better during our days in the mountains.

After my examination, the doctor looked at me sternly. "I believe you are suffering from acute appendicitis. I am sending you by ambulance to our regional hospital for more tests. You likely will need emergency surgery to remove your appendix."

Ruslan and I stared at each other in disbelief. It was almost comical—yet another crisis thwarting our plans.

I had told Ruslan never to let anyone operate on me in Ukraine. Multiple times I had said, "If I'm unconscious, just airlift me out of the country." Most hospitals here are a nightmare in treatment and services. Ukrainian hospitals have the highest infection rate in Europe. Unfortunately, in my situation, a ruptured appendix could have far worse consequences than risking treatment at the local hospital.

At the regional hospital, doctors couldn't say with certainty that it was my appendix. However, out of concern that my appendix would rupture, they recommended surgery. By this time, I was in tears, scared for my life. It seemed we had no choice but to go with whatever the doctors were recommending.

"I know this is not the ideal situation, and I wish we had more options," Ruslan said. "But the nurse told me that the surgeon doing the procedure is considered one of the best in the country."

Ruslan and the girls walked beside me as a nurse pushed me in a wheelchair into the main surgical building. The hospital was huge, the building itself dating back to the late 1800s. It still had outside bomb shelters dug into the ground in various locations. Its appearance was so run down that it looked like it had indeed survived two world wars and the Soviet Union.

Ruslan and the girls prayed over me, and then I was wheeled into a pre-op room where I was told to lie down on a hospital bed and wait until the surgical team came to get me. The room looked like something from a 1950s horror movie. I had two beds to choose from. One was covered in hair, and the other was covered in dried blood. I asked the nurse how she expected me to lie down in such an unsanitary place right before surgery. She gave me a funny look and asked why I hadn't brought my own bed linens. She told me to go to the drugstore and buy some disposable sheets.

I now walked back out to find Ruslan to tell him to find some disposable sheets so that I could lie down and get some rest before my surgery. I spent an hour in that dirty, outdated pre-op room, mostly crying and praying. I decided that if the actual operating room looked like this one, then I was going to refuse the surgery and take my chances elsewhere. But as I was talking to God, an incredible peace came over me. I could feel his comfort in a tangible way, and I was able to doze off for a while.

When the surgical team came to get me, I was directed to lie down on the gurney they had brought so they could roll me into the operating room.

"Do you want me to put on a surgical gown?" I asked.

"No," I was told. "The surgery will be done with you wearing your clothes."

That seemed weird to me, but still feeling peace, I lay on the gurney and was rolled out of the pre-op room. I waved to Ruslan and the girls, who were looking super stressed and worried. I told them I'd see them soon in recovery.

Thankfully, the operating room looked a few decades newer than anywhere else I'd been that day, and I told the surgeon I would try to be a good patient so he could go home to his family before midnight. It was already after eight o'clock by this point. The last thing I remembered was watching the anesthesiologist shoot something into my IV.

Sometime later, in the foggy realms of my brain, I heard a high-pitched voice saying something in Ukrainian. "Shaaarrryynnn! Breathe, Sharyn! Breathe!"

I thought that was a weird thing to say. *Aren't I breathing? Here, let me check.* I took a deep breath and exhaled it. Yep, I was breathing. What seemed like moments later, I opened my eyes and saw a woman looking down at me checking my vitals.

Ruslan and Gloria soon came into the recovery room to see me. It was now about midnight, and Emily was asleep on the couch at the nurses' station. I was a bit loopy and said something silly to Gloria, which made her laugh.

I was wheeled outside and into another hospital building, then carried up two flights of stairs to my hospital room. The room had eight empty beds in it. Since it was so late, the staff graciously allowed Ruslan and the girls to spend the night with me. The beds had no sheets, blankets, or pillows, but after such a harrowing day, we were thankful just to be together.

The next morning, I woke up feeling as if I had been run over by a semitruck. Ruslan informed me that in the middle of my surgery, a nurse came out to the car where he and the girls were waiting and told him to go to the drugstore and buy a surgical gown for the gynecologist, as she was needed to assist in my "in progress" surgery. Ruslan didn't waste time asking why he had to supply the needed surgical gown. He ran to the drugstore to buy one.

Apparently, after opening me up, the surgeon had discovered not appendicitis but a rupturing cyst on one of my ovaries. According to protocol, he had to bring in the gynecologist to confirm the situation before he could remove the cyst. Ruslan also told me that he had talked to the anesthesiologist prior to my surgery and had given her an extra one hundred dollars to make sure I was given the good medicine. He wanted assurances that I would wake up, as stories abounded of doctors using the wrong type or quantities of anesthesia. It was sad we had to pay extra to get the "good" medicine.

I spent seven days in the hospital before my doctor signed the release forms to discharge me. After eighteen years of ministry work in Ukraine, it was the most shocking cultural experience I had endured. My surgical ward had more than fifty patients, with one or two nurses on call at any given hour, running the marathon of trying to administer everyone's medications and deal with everyone's needs. Bathrooms were located on either side of the floor, and for the first three days, it took me more than fifteen minutes to reach one since walking was such a painful and slow-moving process. I tried to ignore the cockroaches scurrying about as I opened the stall in the women's bathroom.

On day two of my recovery, my room was still empty, though all the other rooms on our floor were full. Ruslan guessed that the hospital administration gave me the courtesy of extra space because they feared bad PR from their American patient if they treated me like every other patient.

Gloria joked that we had traded a three-star vacation package for a no-star hospital package. It would have been funny if I hadn't been so miserable. My first forty-eight hours in that hospital were particularly bad. And that bad came after months of awful.

On my third day there, late in the evening and all alone in my room, I told God what I thought of my predicament. *I mean, come on! What else are we going to have to go through this year? God! How can you ask me to have joy in these present sufferings when every single nerve in my body hurts? All I feel is pain. God, none of this is fair. And I'm not just talking about being in the hospital! This isn't how it's supposed to be. I can't do this anymore!*

The pit of pity had enveloped me, and I felt so self-righteous as I pointed it all out to God, as if he didn't see my situation. And in that lonely, quiet place of tears and anger, the Spirit of the Lord filled my empty hospital room, and I heard the clear, quiet voice of the Father. They weren't words of comfort. They were words of reprimand.

Sharyn, open your eyes and see my provision. You have a husband who is taking incredible care of you. You have a family who loves you. You have the financial means to pay for the best that this hospital has to offer. And you have me and my promise to never leave you or forsake you, or to lay before you more than you will be able to handle. Look around, daughter. Look at all that you have been given. You are surrounded by equally ill people who have none of these things. They lie in pain, and they have no hope. Stop feeling sorry for yourself. Look out at a hurting world that is thirsty for a reason to take another step. For however long I keep you here, you know the hope that they seek. Bring my presence into this space.

It wasn't at all the response I sought, but it was exactly what I needed to hear. For months I'd been trying to figure out the *why* behind everything we were going through. Why would God bring such direction and confirmation only to have our lives completed uprooted and thrown into a completely different part of the country? Was there a greater plan somewhere we were supposed to see? How was it all supposed to work itself out for good? There was no answer. But in that holy moment with God, I accepted that I didn't need to know the why. He was asking me just to be faithful. To love a broken world better, because of my own brokenness. To trust him more perfectly in all the unknowns, because either he was faithful, or he wasn't. And I knew, despite all my questions and doubts, that he was faithful.

That night around one o'clock, I hobbled to the bathroom. After using the toilet, I was so exhausted that I just sat there for a while, waiting until I felt I had the strength to make the trek back.

Just as I was getting ready to leave, the door opened, and a cleaning lady walked in. She looked at me with kind eyes and asked, "Are you okay?" She had noticed that I hadn't come back to my room and, since the night-shift nurse was nowhere to be seen, had come to check on me. She walked me back to my room, tucked me into my bed, and told me that if I needed anything at all not to hesitate to ask. I felt as if I had been visited by an angel. Such kindness. I never saw the woman again, whether she indeed was a ministering angel or just got busy cleaning another floor of the hospital. I will never forget her care in a moment when I needed the reminder that I wasn't alone.

The next day, my empty room filled to max capacity with around eight other patients. It wasn't lost on me that in the space of one hour every bed was filled, after days of being empty, and that the space in my heart had opened to engage with others. To my amazement, we all became a team. Whoever was mobile was elected to find the nurse or a family member if something was needed. We shared our stories of what had brought us to the hospital, and for however long, we were community for each other.

It took me a month to physically recover and return to normal activities. Ruslan said that this experience was my initiation into becoming a true Ukrainian. I thought about how so many Ukrainian and Russian words used in everyday conversation had the root word for "health" in them. I wondered if it was because Ukrainians understood that with their medical system, if you didn't have your health, you were in a lot of trouble.

I wish I could say that after my surgery things got better, but the trials of our no good, very bad, truly terrible year were not over yet.

On September 8, our thirteenth wedding anniversary, we invited our neighbors Vadim and Alla and our YWAM Ternopil friends Roman and Rebecca Taturevych out to a celebratory dinner. All our kids were also at the party. I wanted to show our friends that we were out of crisis mode. We were on the mend! No more sickness. No more emergencies. We were turning the corner.

This seemed to be the case—until just moments after our waitress took our order, Gloria came staggering around the corner. Blood poured from a huge gash on her head. She had fallen headfirst off the jungle gym at the playground. I grabbed a pile of napkins, applying pressure to the wound, and off we went to the children's hospital emergency room. Thankfully, Gloria had no trauma to the skull or brain, just a bloody head wound. The attending physician, who looked to be about eighty years old, allowed me to stay with Gloria in the operating room as he sewed up the cut. I asked why Gloria hadn't received any anesthesia, and the doctor said that she was in shock and wouldn't feel anything.

I held Gloria's hand and sang "Jesus Loves the Children of the World" while she lay quietly, bravely enduring the stitching without so much as a whimper. The doctor used only five stitches to sew up what was, in my opinion, a very uneven wound. The doctor said a more cosmetic approach wasn't necessary since Gloria's hair would cover the scar.

Thanksgiving came along, and I once again determined to be on the giving instead of receiving end of people's kindness. I was sure our neighbors must think there was a perpetual cloud of bad luck over our family because it had been one thing after another for the past nine months. I wanted to show them that this time we really had turned the proverbial corner and were ready to engage with the world again. I invited our neighbors over for

Thanksgiving dinner and spent two days preparing for what I wanted to be the nicest Thanksgiving experience I could offer these precious people.

Three hours before our guests were to arrive, we received a phone call from Tamara Statkiewicz, whose family was also on staff with YWAM Ternopil. Tamara has two sons, Sasha and Tolik, and we had just been at their home for a birthday party. She apologetically explained that she had found lice in her sons' hair, and since our kids had been playing together, she wanted me to know just in case.

I hung up the phone and wished she had called me six hours later. Sure enough, we found lice eggs in the girls' long, thick hair. I burst into tears as Ruslan called the neighbors to cancel Thanksgiving dinner. He assured me that they wouldn't be very thankful if we "blessed" them with these little pests and all the combing, zapping, shampooing, and laundry loads that went into getting rid of them.

The grand finale of our terrible, no good, very bad year was my getting a severe case of laryngitis the night before a women's Christmas tea that I had organized. The theme was Emmanuel: God with us. We had nearly sixty women from around Ternopil in attendance. I was the keynote speaker, and I decided that come what may, even with a voice that sounded like a croaking toad, I was going to share a message from my heart with these women. A message about overcoming. A message about hope. The message about Emmanuel—God with us. And I did, raspy voice and all. God didn't take away the discomfort of my voice, but he used me through it anyway. I have come to realize that he will always use whatever we have to offer, even our brokenness—especially our brokenness—as a blessing to others.

In all honesty, 2014 was the year I didn't lose my faith. It was the year that I learned how to "let go and let God." It felt as if the proverbial carpet had been pulled out from under our feet. Nothing was back in place. Nothing was as it should be. Nothing about the future was even remotely clear. We were walking in the dark in that there was no vision for the future; God was simply asking us to put one foot in front of the other and learn how to be faithful with what was important for today.

CHAPTER 12

Lord, Can I Trust You?

I've always thought that one of the most beautiful gifts in the world is the innocence of a child. There is something so pure and precious in the way a child simply trusts. The way a child loves unconditionally. The way a child knows everything will be okay if mom or dad are nearby.

What we had experienced in Ukraine was, for me, a shattering of that innocence in a spiritual sense. I felt as if my childlike trust in God had been ripped from me, and I didn't know what to do with the feelings stirring within me. For the first time in my life, I was asking God, "Are we going to be okay? God, can I trust you?"

I knew God was trustworthy, and yet in the pit of my stomach sat a lump of uncertainty. I wondered again and again, "Are we going to survive this upheaval?" I was upset with myself for feeling angry and discouraged, and yet that was undeniably exactly how I felt. The bottom line was, I wasn't sure if God's version of okay was going to be okay with me.

One of the big questions I carried was how God could have so clearly confirmed our move to start YWAM Sevastopol, only to have that vision demolished by the Russian invasion. Why would God spend so much time pouring vision and passion into us about this new place, only to have those plans shattered? We stubbornly held on to the hope of returning to Crimea but had no idea how that could be possible. When 2014 ended, we were exhausted emotionally and physically, and we decided to return to the USA for a time of rest and to connect with our supporting churches.

Throughout our years of ministry work in Ukraine, we have been blessed to have a group of about ten churches in the US supporting our ministry and family. We've always felt that part of our job as international ministry workers is to be available to spend time with each church—to inspire and encourage them in recognizing that they are a part of all the amazing things God is doing in Eastern Europe. Having grown up in small-town America, I also care about being a window to the world for these believers, many of whom have never been farther than a few hundred miles from home. But as we prepared for our departure, I realized I wasn't ready to tell our story yet. We were still in the storm, and I wasn't sure yet if our boat was going to sink or sail.

We recognized that we needed some time to settle our emotions and, as a family, process our experiences before speaking at our supporting churches. Our solution? To take a three-week road trip. We decided to buy a minivan at an auction in Pennsylvania, then drive down the East Coast, across the southern states, and then back up the West Coast to Idaho. We'd be visiting friends and churches and national parks all along the way.

Our trip through the States was an absolute balm to body, mind, and soul for all four of us. Every day was an adventure as we explored the monuments and museums of Washington, DC, enjoyed the hometown cooking of South Carolina, and rested on the white sandy beaches of Florida. It felt so good to laugh, learn, and talk with the girls about what 2014 had cost us.

We still didn't know where home would be for us. We hoped to return to Crimea one day, but even if we did, our community there was gone. Where would our new life be? Where would our girls finish growing up? As the political situation in Ukraine deteriorated, I wondered if we would ever find our way back home.

About ten days into our trip, we found ourselves in the miles and miles of barren country between Dallas and El Paso. Our plan was to drive until we got tired and then locate a cheap motel along the freeway to spend the night. About five o'clock, we were near Midland, Texas, and decided to see if we could find a place to stay. I expected a night's stay to cost about fifty dollars, which is what we had budgeted. I was shocked to discover that an oil boom in the area had driven up the cost to more than two hundred dollars. So we headed south, hoping to find something cheaper the farther we drove. I began to look up motels advertised on Google. No luck. Everything was too expensive.

About thirty minutes into our search, I began calling motels in Monahans, a town about fifty miles farther down the interstate. My third call on Google's motel list was a place called the Silver Spur. I dialed the number, and a woman with a thick Indian accent answered the phone. I asked her if she had a room with two beds available and how much it would cost. Her answer left me speechless.

"Yes," she said. "I have one room left, and are you the missionary family I've been saving it for?"

I didn't know what to answer. While we were a missionary family, I knew she wasn't saving the room for us, because I had just looked up her motel five minutes ago! On the other hand, what were the chances that there would be two missionary families looking for lodging at the Silver Spur that day?

"Well, ma'am, we are a missionary family, but I'm sure you aren't saving the room for us."

"No, no, come. I'll save the room for you, and it's a good price."

"Okay," I answered, "but I'm sure you are saving that room for someone else. I wouldn't want to take someone else's reservation."

I disconnected the call and looked at Ruslan and the girls as goose bumps rose on my arms. "Um, I'm not sure what is happening, but I think God wants us to go to the Silver Spur Motel in Monahans. Apparently, they've been saving the last room—for us!"

When we arrived at the Silver Spur Motel, our first impression was not good. The cinder-block structure was right next to train tracks, and the building looked so worn down on the outside that we shuddered to think about the conditions inside. There were boarded-up businesses on either side of the motel, and to be honest, the Silver Spur looked to be the only sign of life on the street.

We thought we should see if any other lodging places were available, but as we started to leave, the sky opened up and it poured rain.

I looked at Ruslan and said, "I wonder if God is asking us to look at the Silver Spur with spiritual eyes, not with our physical ones."

We decided that if we didn't find anything under one hundred dollars, this would be our sign to go back. As we drove up to a much nicer-looking hotel near the interstate, Ruslan turned into what he thought was the parking lot. Instead, he hit a curb, and we all were thrown forward. We laughed and wondered if God was literally stopping us from going that direction. When Ruslan went into the hotel, the cost for a night was well over two hundred dollars.

We turned around and drove back to the Silver Spur. In the motel office I noticed a picture of the Taj Mahal on the wall and a second picture of Jesus holding a lamb.

An Indian woman walked into the office and immediately asked, "Are you the missionary family I have been waiting for?"

We all smiled in amazement, and I answered, "We are a missionary family, but how did you know that we were coming? We didn't even know we were coming until sixty minutes ago!"

"I got a call this morning telling me that there would be a missionary family staying tonight and to save them a room," she replied. "So I've been saving our last room for you, and it's ready!"

I looked over at Emily, and her eyes reflected the same thing I'm sure we were all thinking. How could this be? Was this a miracle unfolding before our eyes? Who could have called for us? And how could they have known that we would be in Monahans?

As she walked us to our room, this sweet woman began to share about her life as a devout Hindu. She was living in England when she had an accident that broke her back. After her surgery, she was recovering at home and was in a lot of pain, barely able to move. One day as she lay in bed, she was flipping through the television channels and came upon a televangelist talking about Jesus. He shared stories of miraculous healings.

"He can heal!" the televangelist said. "Jesus loves all people and cares about you. Call on the name of Jesus today!"

Hindus believe in all sorts of gods, so the woman thought to herself, *Why not pray in the name of this Jesus and see what happens?* And so she prayed for her back to be healed, and right there, she experienced an instantaneous healing. She met Jesus the Healer, gave her life to him, and somehow or another found herself in the middle of nowhere, Texas, running the Silver Spur.

As she came to the end of her story, she looked at us and said, "I have a prayer ministry here. I pray for all the people who stay here. Truck drivers, road trippers, anyone who spends the night gets prayed for. I've seen many people give their hearts to Jesus. God has healed people from cancer. He does miracles here all the time."

We stood there amazed at her story. That's when she looked at us and asked, "Is there anything I could pray about for you?"

In that moment, I felt the fear around my heart begin to ease as the presence of God surrounded us with warmth. We shared a little bit about our story and humbly asked her just to pray for us. And right there, in the middle of that broken-down, boarded-up street in Texas, God met us.

As this precious sister prayed for us, without any idea what we were carrying, she prayed the most beautiful, powerful prayer. We felt the presence of the Holy Spirit fall around us, and I heard the Lord whisper to me, *There is nowhere on planet Earth that I do not have my ministering angels ready to help you in every and any need. I was there. I am here. I am with you. Always.*

That evening for the first time in a long time, I felt genuine hope that we were going to be okay. God had brought a woman from north Idaho, a man from Ukraine, two young girls, and a sister from India together in a West Texas parking lot so that he could begin to heal our brokenness. I could almost see the presence of God and his angels surrounding the place. It was the dirtiest, loudest, most run-down place we'd ever stayed in, but we were exactly where the Lord wanted us to be. After all, he had called ahead to make our reservation.

The next morning as we prepared to leave, we saw no sign of any other missionary family and no sign of the Indian woman. We left a note of thanks and goodbye and headed west on the interstate. Two hours later, we stopped to fill up the gas tank on the outskirts of El Paso and discovered that our radiator was leaking. Ruslan guessed it was the result of our run-in with the curb the past evening. We got directions to a nearby auto shop, and twenty minutes later, we were all comfortably settled in the waiting room as the mechanic fixed the minivan's cracked radiator.

As a homeschool educator, I often joke about all the "classrooms" our girls have experienced over the years. They have done their schoolwork on trains, on planes, at border crossings, on road trips, in beauty salons, at conferences in various countries—and on this day at an auto repair shop in El Paso.

As we waited, I thought about our experience the night before. The Lord had used that precious Indian woman to answer my "God, can I trust you?" question. I felt he was asking me not to look at all the problems but just to look at Jesus. He cared about our lives. He cared about our pain. He would work things out for our good, even if we couldn't see it yet. I finally felt able to receive this truth.

As my tears began to flow, I noticed a picture on the wall. It was a beautifully framed and decorated image of Proverbs 3:5–6, which says, "Trust in the Lord with all your heart and lean not on your own understanding; in all your ways submit to him, and he will make your paths straight." Even in the waiting room of an auto repair shop in West Texas, God was leading us.

About four days later, we had made our way north to visit the Grand Canyon and then had one more day to explore the red-rock buttes of Sedona, Arizona.

We decided to spend the afternoon hiking near Cathedral Rock, and we weren't disappointed. We picnicked in a little meadow looking up at the towering rock butte and just enjoyed the beauty of God's creation. When it came time to leave, we drove about a mile down the road until we came to an overlook where we stopped and stared at the incredible view of the area where we had spent our day. The sun was setting, and the reddish hues of the rocks glistened. Again, we felt a holy moment fall over our family. We took time to pray, and we heard the Lord speak to us.

As we stared out at enormous Cathedral Rock sticking up from the desert floor, the Lord reminded us, *I am bigger than Cathedral Rock. I am bigger than Putin. I am bigger than political upheaval. I am bigger than every problem you face. When you look at me, Goliath becomes just a speck of dust. Keep your eyes on me, for I am able.*

Over the next six months, we visited churches and supporters. Each time, our story of holding on to Jesus during the toughest time of our lives was giving hope to others. Many were walking through their own rough times, wrestling with their own questions. Our story gave them hope, showing how beautiful it is to be part of God's redemptive story.

That summer we also enjoyed special times with my parents at Priest Lake, Idaho. In September the girls started second and fourth grades at House of the Lord Christian Academy, and we made plans to return to Ukraine.

Later that month, we did a five-day debriefing at YWAM Montana to help us process the events of the past year. Debriefing helps people process the impact of a past event. It's a healthy exercise for anyone, but especially powerful for those who have been through a traumatic experience. Part of our debrief homework was to create a timeline of the events we had experienced and to note when we had encountered crisis, conflict, concern, change, or criticism. On the fourth day, our debriefing team directed us to review our timeline and answer the question, "Where was God during each experience?" As I prayed through all the big moments of 2014, I couldn't believe what I saw. It was as if blinders had been lifted from my eyes. I could see how God—with amazing care—had been intervening for, engaging with, protecting, and leading us in every moment. God was there; he was there *huge*. He was there in the hardest, most agonizing moments. He opened doors and provided answers. He brought people into our lives just when we needed them.

With the perspective of time and space, I was able to see that not only was God there, he was actively there. I could finally see that in the most horrible, painful year of our lives, God had carried us. He had tenderly loved us. Provided for us. And that day as I looked back, I could hear him whisper, *Beloved, don't give up. Keep your eyes on me. I'm already working on your behalf in places you don't even know about yet. It's going to be okay. It's going to be okay. It's going to be okay.*

Finally, I was able to say with my whole heart, "Jesus, I trust you."

Cathedral Rock, Sedona, Arizona, 2015
Our reminder that God is bigger than everything we face!

CHAPTER 13

In Search of Home

We returned to Ukraine just a few weeks before the second anniversary of our evacuation from Crimea. Russia continued to occupy the area we once called home, and political tensions remained high. We longed to go back there and fulfill the vision God had given us. We still had our house in Simferopol, where most of our possessions gathered dust. But returning to Crimea at present seemed an impossible dream. So we camped out in our Ternopil townhouse, struggling to find where God wanted us to be for the long term.

YWAM Ternopil provided us with a wonderful community, and we busied ourselves with a variety of ministry projects, including a family club we started called Bloom. Our hope was that God would use us to help local families grow and blossom in their relationships.

One highlight of Bloom's outreach was Marriage Week, a YWAM-led international movement started by Richard and Maria Kane in 1996. Marriage Week is currently active in more than twenty-four countries around the world and commits each year to programs designed to celebrate traditional marriage and promote tools to help married couples be successful.

Ruslan and I loved the idea of starting a Marriage Week in Ternopil. We envisioned a week of events that would promote marriage and help build strong families. However, since we were new to the area, we didn't have the connections to promote the idea on a citywide level.

Thankfully, God helped us overcome that hurdle through a citywide pastors' breakfast started by YWAM Ternopil. The monthly breakfast brought together pastors from various denominations for fellowship and prayer. This was no small thing. Historically, the Catholic, Orthodox, Baptist, Pentecostal, and other churches of Ternopil declined to work with one another. Since YWAM is interdenominational, it provides a neutral territory for pastors from these denominations to meet.

Ruslan and I were invited share our plan for Marriage Week at the pastors' breakfast. We introduced ourselves, shared a bit of our story, and invited these pastors to consider partnering with us as we put on the first-ever Marriage Week in Ternopil. The response was amazing! These pastors not only liked the idea, they also wanted to get involved. Suddenly we went from being the couple nobody knew to sharing about Marriage Week around the city.

Marriage Week, which took place in May 2016, was the first time in Ternopil history that churches worked together, across denominations, on the same event. We discovered that supporting traditional marriage was something we could all get behind. Thanks to the churches' support, we organized a citywide parade that attracted more than a thousand people. It marched through downtown Ternopil with an orchestra and big signs encouraging couples to stay the course. We held a family festival with carnival games in one of the city parks and a couples' café, where we served tea and cookies while couples discussed prearranged questions pertaining to family life and marriage. We also held a competition to find the longest-married couple and came across Andriy Romanovich and Ludmilla Ivanovna, who had been married for sixty-nine years. We invited the media, and over tea and coffee in a local café, this couple talked about what had helped them grow a marriage for almost seven decades.

"What's your secret to staying married for so long?" a journalist asked Ludmilla.

"Cooking three tasty meals per day," she answered.

"What about you?" the journalist asked, turning the mike over to the husband.

"You just keep coming home every day," Andriy said with a chuckle.

The interview even made the national media channels. Our hope was that this week would inspire churches to promote other marriage programs all year.

Though Crimea was on our hearts and minds daily, at least we had found a way to be a blessing to Ternopil.

While in Ternopil, we looked for an opportunity to visit the nearby Carpathian Mountains. We kept hearing how beautiful they were. Our previous mountain vacation had been prevented by my emergency surgery. So in June, we made new plans to visit the area. We chose to stay in Yablunitsa, a town we were told had stunning mountain views. Growing up in the mountains of Idaho, I loved being outdoors. Hiking, biking, and playing in mountain lakes was my childhood, and I wondered how the Carpathians would compare.

As we drove, it felt as if we were in the Alps, somewhere straight out of Johanna Spyri's *Heidi,* with high Alpine meadows stretching farther than any road could reach. The Carpathian Mountains had young conifer forests and fast-flowing rivers that reminded me of home. The houses were beautiful with their wooden artistry and carved window frames and roof details. The churches also were built from wood and sat close to the ground, their cupolas glistening with golden metal. The locals, known as the Hutsul people, spoke with an accent and mixed in Hungarian words. Even their dress attested to a culture that had managed to preserve its heritage during Soviet occupation.

As we arrived at our hotel, we were all breathless at the beauty of these mountains. Every direction we looked were meadows covered with vibrant wildflowers that transformed the grassy fields into soft blankets of blues, reds, yellows, and purples. In the distance, the two largest mountains in Ukraine—Petros and Hoverla—created a panorama that I could have stared at all day long. The village looked as if it hadn't changed in a hundred years, with sheep and goats in the pastures and villagers plowing their fields behind mules and horses. This little Carpathian village was one of the most beautiful places we had ever been.

That spring we had received a tax return of around six thousand dollars. We wondered if that money might be enough to purchase a little piece of land in this village. It was a spontaneous thought, but at a small produce stand we asked if there was anything for sale in the village. The vendor gave us a phone number, and when Ruslan called to inquire, he received an invitation to tea.

Misha and Svetlana, a couple older than Ruslan and me, greeted our family warmly.

"We've been watching your sweet family walk past our home these last few days. What a delight to have you in our home for tea!" Svetlana said, as she laid out a feast of homemade cooking.

"We didn't come here thinking to buy any property," Ruslan explained, "but your village and the mountain views are so beautiful, we couldn't help but inquire as to properties for sale. Maybe we can build a cabin one day and become a little part of this village."

After tea, Misha drove us up the mountain to show us the land he had for sale.

When we stepped out of his car, I almost fell over. The quarter-acre lot sat by itself overlooking the Carpathian Mountains. We could see for miles, and the view touched a place in my heart. We saw the extravagant, incredible, pristine touches of a Creator who had taken extra time on this little mountaintop. When we learned that the lot was in our price range, it didn't take us long to start the purchase process.

We thought of this land as an investment for the future. Maybe in time we could build a small home there. But there was a little flutter inside me that made me wonder if the Lord was doing something more. It felt good to have a project like this. A place to get to know better.

As we returned from our wonderful mountain vacation and spring turned into early summer, our big questions about our future still loomed. Where would "home" be for us? Was it possible to go back home to Crimea, and if not, where would we go?

In my heart, choosing anything besides Crimea felt like giving up. Almost defensively, we sometimes told people that Crimea was our home, and even though we hadn't set foot there in two years, I longed to return and continue our ministry there. Yet we had no clear direction for the future. God was still asking us to be faithful in the day to day and to trust him with all our unanswered questions. Once again, I was aware that God was training us to trust him with our big picture. To trust him with our dreams and hopes.

We decided to give ourselves one more year to decide about Crimea. We reasoned that by that point, the way back would be clear or it would be closed. Either way, we knew we needed to move in some direction, to reestablish home for our family and put down roots somewhere. We also recognized that we needed to make a trip to Crimea. How else could we determine if it was even possible for YWAM to still exist there?

Planning our return, however brief, was much easier said than done. In the aftermath of the occupation, the world had implemented sanctions on Russia and even stricter restrictions on Crimea. It wasn't possible to fly into Crimea from anywhere except Russia. The trains between Ukraine and Crimea were closed. Crimea's banking system, along with the ability to send or receive money, was cut off from every country except Russia. It wasn't possible to ship things in or out of Crimea, and we heard horror stories from people who tried to cross the border into Ukraine with their valuables.

The other problem with getting into Crimea was me. The only way into Crimea from Ukraine was to walk or drive across the border, and it was a tedious process even for Ukrainian-passport holders. We had no idea what it would be like for a foreigner like me. We didn't know a single person without a Ukrainian passport who had even tried to cross the border.

We contacted our regional authority and explained our situation. The staff assured us that, to the best of their knowledge, any permanent resident of Ukraine (which I was) would be allowed through on the Ukrainian side. A Russian visa was required to cross through on the Russian side. We set about making all the necessary preparations, and finally in July, we left by car for the two-day trip to the border.

We were so excited. Although Crimea was occupied territory, life on the peninsula still moved in its usual ways. Residents went to work and to school, swam in the Black Sea, and enjoyed the peninsula's beautiful landscapes. We were eager to see friends who still lived in Crimea, and we also were looking forward to being back in our house. As the pieces began to fall into place, I cautiously carried hope in my heart that this trip would be our first step in moving back home.

We brought our friend Yana with us. She was on staff with YWAM Ternopil and was originally from Kazakhstan. With the same permanent residence permit I had, she was looking forward to spending some vacation days in Crimea, and we were excited to show her our favorite places.

However, as we approached the first border crossing, the reality of the situation began to sink in. I had never seen a war zone before. The border crossing was in the middle of a field, with barbed wire stretched out on either side as far as I could see. Near the crossing were concrete guard posts with openings just big enough for pointing and shooting a weapon. Large cement obstacles, like enormous jacks from the classic game I played as a kid, littered the sides of the road.

We pulled up to the first checkpoint on the Ukrainian side, and as Ruslan stepped out with our pile of documents, we waited and prayed. Moments later, he came back with news we didn't want.

First, Yana would not be allowed to enter. As a citizen of Kazakhstan, even with Ukrainian permanent residence status, she was not permitted to cross into Crimea. Second, the situation looked to be the same for me. However, we were encouraged to go to the nearby city of Kherson and inquire there. The fact that we owned property in Crimea might allow us to apply for a special short-term permit that would allow me entrance. The girls were free to go through, if Ruslan was with them, as they were considered Ukrainian citizens.

Discouraged, but not ready to give up, we turned around and drove an hour back to Kherson, where we made our way to the regional foreign office. We explained our situation—that we hadn't been home in two years, that we had driven four hundred miles to get there—and asked what we could do to get through. After many hours of waiting, someone explained to us that yes, I could get in because of my marriage to Ruslan and our ownership of a house in Crimea. But unfortunately, they discovered that my first name on my Ukrainian marriage certificate had been translated one letter differently from my first name on my permanent residency document. That mistake would have to be fixed way back in Lutsk, where I was registered. They would not be able to process the travel permit until I had fixed this mistake. It was unbelievable to me. One letter in my name kept us from being able to go home.

"Please," I said, tears glistening in my eyes. "I know I have a passport from another country, but Crimea is our home. It's just one letter. Are you sure there isn't a way for us to be able to have this homecoming?"

"I'm so sorry for your situation," the customs agent replied, "but this is our protocol. The translation of your name needs to be the same on all your documents for us to accept your transit papers."

There would be no homecoming for us that summer. We drove instead to a village called Zhelezny Port to have some days to rest at a seaside guesthouse. Ruslan left the next day to see if he could get through the border. On the Russian side, he was informed that our car would not be allowed through because he didn't have the correct vehicle registration. So Ruslan turned around once again and joined us at the beach.

As we made our way back to Ternopil, we realized that we had actually made some progress. Now we knew what to do to get our whole family into Crimea. We knew how to get our car into Crimea. We knew what even our local authorities hadn't known. Getting that information had required driving a thousand miles round trip, but now we had it. We began the paperwork process and made plans to try again in the fall.

In October, we set out for Crimea once again, and this time we made it all the way through the border. We spent three weeks in our house, seeing our friends and having a wonderful time. However, being in Crimea felt different. Every time we asked someone about moving back, the answer was the same. They had no idea how we could live there and work with YWAM or any other organization. Some thought it unwise even to try.

It was encouraging, however, to see that the church in Crimea was growing despite harsh new restrictions on religious institutions. We took part in a baptism celebration in which twenty people confirmed their decision to follow Jesus. More than fifty people had gathered to witness the occasion and to have a time of worship and a barbecue. All of this, of course, was illegal according to the laws of Russia, and yet as the pastor said, "If you get arrested for sharing your faith, I'll come bail you out!"

When our three-week stay was over and it was time to depart from Simferopol, we set out at 4:00 a.m. and arrived at the border with our van crammed with everything we could shove into it. Border guards made us unload every box, suitcase, backpack, and handbag in the van so that they could open and inspect each one. The guards were civil and professional, but the process from start to finish took more than four hours.

On the drive back, we took a short detour to the industrial city of Mariupol, only twenty-five miles from the Russian border on the Sea of Azov. Mariupol was an active military zone, but the more we had prayed about bringing our children there, the more we had felt peace about stopping. This city had come under attack at the onset of the war. The Kremlin had wanted to take Mariupol, but the Ukrainian army pushed them back. The front lines were still close enough that residents could hear bombs blasting day and night. Hundreds of thousands of refugees from the Donbas region had sought refuge in Mariupol. We had a connection with a local Baptist church in the city and wanted to see how we might partner with them to help support this displaced community.

The girls, now ages eight and ten, were eager to help. Although we had not had our home bombed, we knew what it felt like to be displaced. Many of the homes we visited didn't have running water, and the cooking had to be done outside over a fire pit. Several homes were inhabited by single moms who had small children, and the vulnerability of their situation was abundantly clear. It blessed my heart to see our children bring food to these precious people, pray with them, and play with their children.

The morning of our departure, we woke up to the sound of muffled explosions in the distance. A ceasefire agreement brokered in Belarus apparently was breached, and the battle was resuming.

As we left Mariupol, the news reported a winter storm warning for western Ukraine. We stopped for the night in Uman, just 250 miles from Ternopil. The next morning, YWAM Ternopil director Lance Roberts called to say that more than three feet of snow had fallen overnight and the highways were a nightmare. He suggested we spend another night in Uman. However, after almost a month away, we were anxious to return. We decided to try to make it all the way home.

Normally this drive is six hours long, but three hours into it, we hit the snow line. Lance was right; the roads were terrible. There were miles of semitrucks stuck along the highway. We came to sections that were completely impassable, and we had to be very creative to find our way around to the other side. After fourteen hours of travel, we were just fifteen miles away from Ternopil, only to discover that the highway was blocked. Determined to make it home, we found a village that allowed us to get around the blocked highway. An hour later we finally turned onto the street that led to our townhouse. There, one block away from our house, our car got stuck in the snow. Our neighbors saw our dilemma and helped push the van the last few meters into our carport. What an adventure we'd had. I was proud of us for beating the odds and making it all the way back to Ternopil. I hoped that the same would be true about our ability to return to Crimea.

Our girls, together with their best friends Annabella and Elizabeth Taturevych, at the Marriage Week parade, Ternopil, Ukraine, 2016

Ruslan and Emily on our property in Yablunitsa, Ukraine, in the Carpathian Mountains. Two of the largest mountains in Ukraine are seen in the background, Hoverla and Petros.

An armored vehicle and roadblock materials on the highway to Mariupol, 2016

CHAPTER 14

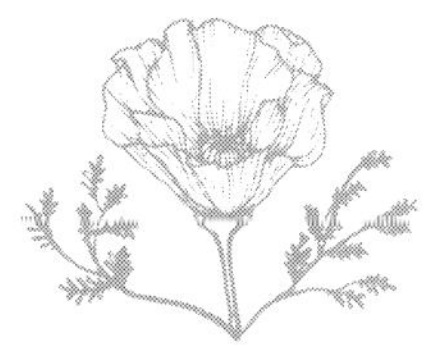

Friendship and Fresh Vision

For now, Ternopil was home base—even though it often didn't feel that way. We still weren't ready to let go of a return to Crimea, but for now returning home to Simferopol just wasn't an option. We continued to put one foot in front of the other, trusting God to guide us.

As we moved into a new school year in the fall of 2016, one huge blessing for us was the development of a home education partnership with the Taturevych family. Roman and Rebecca Taturevych, together with their kids Elizabeth, Annabella, and Nathaniel, had worked with YWAM in Ternopil since the 1990s.

Our girls were the same ages as their daughters, and they became inseparable friends. Rebecca and I often joked that God used a similar blueprint for our lives. Though we didn't meet until 2002, we grew up eighty-four miles from each other. As teenagers we both worked summers as lifeguards, participated in the Junior Miss program, and attended Seattle Pacific University. We both did a Discipleship Training School, went on outreach to Ukraine, and met and married Ukrainian husbands. We also discovered that two of our daughters were born thirteen days apart in neighboring hospitals. This unexpected friendship was one of the great gifts of our coming to Ternopil.

When we arrived in Ternopil in February 2014, I did the best I could to get Gloria and Emily through to the end of the school year. That fall, I taught homeschool classes in the storage room at the YWAM base. Throughout that year, I pitched to Roman and Rebecca the idea of forming a homeschool cooperative. I was thrilled when they said yes, and we started working together.

In many European countries, home education is against the law. Thankfully this is not the case in Ukraine, though most Ukrainian parents still consider it strange. Their many questions have created a great platform for me to share my passion for education. I often tell parents that it is our God-given mandate to educate our children. Whether we choose the instrument of public school, private school, or homeschool, it is our responsibility to be involved in the process and the policy making. We should never assume that good education is happening in our child's classroom; rather, we should learn about the curriculum and teaching methods. This is so important because teachers don't just convey knowledge about math, reading, and science; they are role models. In reality, they are discipling our children. This vision for the God-ordained role of parents in their children's education is something I was grateful to have the opportunity to share with families in Ternopil.

With the school year well underway, in February 2017 Rebecca and I participated in a women's retreat in beautiful Málaga, Spain. What a joy to land in seventy-degree Málaga after leaving below-zero weather in Ukraine. When we arrived at the villa that hosted our retreat, there were orange trees everywhere—and they were ripe for the picking! We were encouraged to eat as many as we wanted. I never knew what a ripe orange was supposed to taste like until I ate one that day. And I couldn't eat just one. They were so juicy and sweet that I ate a whole pile of them.

I decided to use this time away to seek God about our future, for the same questions were still pressing. Were we going back? Were we staying in Ternopil? Was God sending us somewhere else? If we were to stay in Ternopil, then why? With our experience in Family Ministries, we could go anywhere in the world and have an effective ministry. If God was going to keep us in Ternopil, I wanted to know why there and not somewhere else. But maybe the hardest "why" question of all was the one that had nothing to do with our future.

God, why would you have seemingly swung wide the door of vision and opportunity in Sevastopol only to have it slammed back in our faces? I wasn't sure I could give up Crimea until I understood the answer to that question.

One thing that I have seen over and over through the years is that whenever you set aside time to spend with Jesus, he takes full advantage. There in Málaga, it seemed that every time I sat down to pray or write in my journal, the Lord was sitting right next to me. He was talking to me, bringing me revelation, gently disciplining me, and lovingly helping me to move past an area where I was stuck.

One morning I asked God to move heaven and earth so we could return to Crimea. I cried out to him, asking why he wasn't speaking to us about the future. I told him how stuck I felt, like we were neither here nor there, and how I felt mounting pressure to decide.

As I sat and listened in the morning stillness, I felt the whisper of his voice. *You aren't open to hearing what I have to say.*

What? As I continued to pray, I saw a picture of myself, arms crossed and my whole posture closed to any topic except returning to Crimea. My heavenly Father was wanting so much to dream with me and share with me, and in essence, I was saying no to the invitation. I wanted him to speak—but only on my terms. Now he was asking me to come before him with an open posture. To allow him to lead the conversation. Then we could talk about the future.

I was shocked at this revelation. I recognized that I had been trying to direct God, not the other way around. I felt that Jesus was asking if I would entrust back to him the burden we carried for Crimea—the love that he had given us for that land and its people. If I was ever going to be open to the Lord's leading in this day of our lives, then I needed to release to Jesus the dream of Crimea ever being "home" again. It didn't mean I was giving up; it meant that I was laying down what I had been holding on to so tightly, entrusting to God the timing and future of our ever returning to Crimea. There wasn't a clear answer to my "why" questions, but there was peace in giving all the things I couldn't understand, the whys and why-nots, back to Jesus. He understood how precious Crimea was to me, because it was precious to him too.

I felt the Holy Spirit say that he was repositioning us for a season. Instead of feeling sadness, I felt expectancy. I remembered our time in the

Carpathians. I saw a cabin being built, a place where pastors and missionaries came to rest and receive ministry.

The next day, our last at the retreat, the participants spread out in various places outside along the terrace, and each member of the ministry team came and prayed for us one at a time. One woman who didn't know anything about my story began to pray for me, saying, "I see a cabin in the mountains with scaffolding on the sides and multitudes of people coming to receive ministry in that location."

I was shocked. It was almost word for word what I had seen in prayer the day before. When I called Ruslan that evening to tell him what had happened, he also felt great peace. He said that as he had been praying, he felt the Lord say, "Freedom!" Freedom to move forward and out of the holding pattern. It had taken us three years, but finally we felt released to cleave to a new territory.

Upon my return to Ternopil, we began to move right away with this new release from the Lord. One of the first things on our minds was where to establish home. If we could sell our home in occupied Crimea—which was a big if—could we use those funds to buy or build a house of our own?

As we began to pray, we felt that the Lord told us we needed to leave Crimea and cleave to Ternopil in the spiritual sense. The leaving would require going back to Simferopol to bid farewell to the life we had known there and prepare our house for sale. We felt the cleaving would be accomplished through the process of building a house. Though it would be much easier just to buy a house, we felt very strongly that God was saying to build and that, through the process of building, we would bond with the land and the people.

Ruslan recalled a conversation he'd had more than a year before with our friend Vitalik, who was trying to sell some property. Vitalik had since moved to the other side of the country, and we hadn't talked to him in some time. Ruslan couldn't remember exactly where the land was, but he knew the general area. On a whim he drove out to have a look around this part of town, hoping he might be able to find the location. He came home later having enjoyed his drive, but not having found the plot of land.

The next day, while Ruslan was out running errands, he called me.

"Sharyn," Ruslan said, "you'll never believe who phoned me today—Vitalik! Totally out of the blue! He invited me to meet him for coffee. This is less than twelve hours after I was out trying to find the property he had for sale. I asked him if it was still for sale, and he said yes. I'm standing on it now, and you have got to come see it!"

An hour later, Ruslan, the girls, and I were standing on a little hill overlooking a beautiful village, just half a mile from the Ternopil city limits. The view was breathtaking. We could hear the gurgle of a creek running through the meadow, and farm animals were out enjoying the first greens of spring. It was love at first sight for all of us. This was going to be our home. I closed my eyes and could see Thanksgiving and Christmas and other events here.

So, less than two weeks after my return from Spain, we started the process of buying land and officially joining the staff at the YWAM Ternopil base. For the first time in three years, we began to dream again about the future. We recognized that building a house and a retreat center in the Carpathians was a huge leap of faith—an endeavor that would take time, expertise, and money. I felt great confidence that God would provide for us, but I was unprepared to say how much money was needed. I had no experience managing a project like this. I needed financial and management guidance, and I began studying these topics.

However, my attention was soon diverted. Late one evening, a Skype number rang on my phone. The only people who ever called me via Skype were in the States, so I hurried to answer the call. It was my aunt JoAnn, my dad's sister.

"Honey," she said, "your dad has had a heart attack. It's bad. You need to get here as soon as possible."

I had heard people talk about getting an emergency, middle-of-the-night phone call, but I had never received one before. Panic, disbelief, and grief hit me like a punch in the gut. I went into action mode, first contacting my mom. She had been diagnosed with early-onset dementia in 2015, and although she was still in control of her mind, navigating such a crisis would be a challenge. To complicate things further, Dad and Mom were wintering in their RV in Arizona. The community there was unknown to me. A kind neighbor had taken Mom under his wing and was helping her get to and from the hospital until I or one of my brothers could get there.

My next call was to the hospital. Dad's doctor told me Dad had suffered a massive heart attack and was unlikely to recover. He said the next forty-eight hours would be critical. Dad had just turned seventy, and he had seemed fine when I talked to him a few days before. It was hard to fathom that a machine was now keeping him alive.

The next challenge was getting to the States. I wanted to be on the next flight out, but Ruslan was traveling, and the girls didn't want me to leave until he got home. We finally decided that the four of us would fly out together. It took three days to arrange our departure, and I had three mostly sleepless nights. I kept thinking I would get a phone call saying Dad had passed. I also hated that my mom was there without family to support her.

Of all our trips back and forth across the Atlantic Ocean, this was the worst. We took the overnight train from Ternopil to Kyiv, then an early-morning flight from Kyiv to Amsterdam. On our flight to the US, a medical emergency forced the pilot to turn around and land in Ireland. There we sat in the airplane for five restless hours. By the time we landed in Chicago, we had missed our connecting flight, so we rebooked our flight to Phoenix, rented a car when we got there, and drove three hours to Lake Havasu City. There we connected with my mom and my brother Corey, who had arrived with his wife, Jen, that morning.

Before entering the hospital, I took a moment with Ruslan and the girls to express what was on my heart. "Guys, I feel like life is about to change in a big way. I can't tell you what it means that we can go through what is coming together."

"We're a team, Mom," Emily assured me. "We're all in this together." Ruslan and Gloria nodded affirmingly.

I knew life was about to change for our team. I just didn't know how much.

Dad was unresponsive when we arrived, but his spirit was still present. I kissed his forehead and whispered words of love and greeting. Though he didn't respond, it felt so good to hold his hand and talk to him. We had always been close, and there was nothing left unsaid between us. I just sat there and thanked God for this man who had loved me since the earliest moments of my life. He taught me to ride a bike, to waterski, and to drive a car. He always made me feel like I was his pride and joy. I couldn't imagine life without him, even though I knew that reality was approaching.

Dad went home to heaven the next day. Mom, Corey, Ruslan, and I were in the room as he passed. We prayed over him, read Scripture to him, and hugged and held each other.

After making funeral arrangements, we rented a minivan and loaded up Mom, her black Labrador, her cat, and as many of her possessions as we could fit for the two-day drive home to Idaho. The cat yowled all the way home, and the girls constantly moaned about dog drool.

Once back in Idaho, we decided we would move in with Mom and stay through the summer. We wanted to do all we could to help her get adjusted to life as a widow. I was so thankful yet again for our relationship with House of the Lord Christian Academy, as it was always such a seamless transition for our girls to reconnect with their classmates and teachers.

I was blown away by all the paperwork Mom had to do to get her financial affairs in order. Helping her with this huge task was a lot of work, but it was also an honor to help manage my parents' legacy. Though Mom's memory was a little slow at times, she was adjusting well. She loved being outdoors with her dog and snuggling with her kitty at night. She loved being around her granddaughters and spending time with my brothers, Corey and Rob, and their kids. With a little bit of help, I thought she would be able to manage life on her own through the next year.

Ruslan returned to Ukraine in mid-April, as we had several ministry engagements that required at least one of us to be on the ground there. Six weeks after Ruslan's departure, he was heading back to Spokane to meet us. It was the longest we had ever been apart.

As the girls and I drove to pick up Ruslan at the Spokane airport that evening, we saw a large moose meandering along the highway. It wasn't hindering traffic, but I kept my eye on it, just in case. Suddenly, something spooked it, and it took off at a gallop right into oncoming traffic. As if in slow motion, the girls and I watched in horror as a sedan coming toward us hit the moose head on. The moose exploded as if a bomb had gone off inside it. The sedan swerved onto our side of the highway, narrowly missed us, and crashed into the trees behind us.

As I pulled over and called 911, I tried to decide what I should do. I felt the urge to go and pray over the woman, but I was sure she had to be either dead or dying. Digging deep for some courage, I told the girls to wait in the car. I hurried over to the sedan wreckage. To my surprise, the woman who had been driving was sitting alongside the road—covered with moose guts, but otherwise uninjured.

Honestly, it was a miracle. When I looked at what was left of the moose and the remains of this woman's car, I couldn't believe that she wasn't seriously hurt—or worse. Her husband was standing nearby; he had been following her in a truck and had seen the whole thing.

As the emergency vehicles arrived, I walked back to the car to tell the girls what had happened. With all the crises we had been through over the past few years, I recognized the rush of adrenaline that had engulfed us. *Lord*, I prayed, *why are we always in crisis? Of all the people who were driving on this highway, why did it have to be the girls and me who were closest to see this terrible accident?*

I heard the Lord say in his quiet voice, *Because I knew you would pray.*

That experience changed my whole outlook on crisis. The moment we realized that the moose was going to get hit by a car, the girls and I started praying. We didn't have to tell each other to pray; it was our automatic response. Seconds before impact, I heard the girls ask God to protect the driver. Could our prayers have released something in the heavenly realms that was the difference between life and death for this woman? Was it possible that I was looking at crisis in the wrong way?

For the first time, instead of feeling like we were crisis magnets, I felt incredibly honored that my daughters and I could be the first on the scene—in prayer. As we ended our time with my mom, helping equip her for the months ahead, and turned our faces back to Ukraine, this was a paradigm shift I would definitely need.

CHAPTER 15

No Longer Displaced

During a fall retreat in the Carpathian Mountains, we were officially prayed in as full-time staff with YWAM Ternopil. It felt incredibly meaningful that this happened near our property, which we prayed God would use one day for a retreat center. Our posture was fully open to God's leading, and it was lovely to see a bit farther down the road of possibilities.

A few weeks later, a short-term missions team arrived for their outreach. All of us—staff and students—were sitting together in our community room, introducing ourselves and saying where we were from. I wondered what our young daughters would say as they prepared to answer this question.

Many people don't think about the significance of the "Where are you from?" question. When you travel as much as we do, we get asked that question a lot, and our answer gives meaning to who we are. Ruslan always answers that he is from Lutsk, Ukraine, because that is his hometown. I say I am from Idaho in the USA. Neither Ruslan nor I have lived in Lutsk or Idaho for more than twenty years. They are not the places we live any longer, but they will always be where we are from. Up until now, our girls had always answered that they were from Crimea. As insignificant as this little moment of introduction seemed on the surface, I wondered if our girls were ready to claim Ternopil as home.

Emily, who was ten years old at the time, scooted a little closer to me and whispered, "Mom, do you think it would be okay if I said I am from Ternopil?"

I looked at Gloria before I answered and saw reflected on her face the same question. With a lump in my throat, I replied, "I think it would be more than okay, Emily, to say you are from Ternopil, because this is where our home is now."

When it was Emily's turn, it was as if she couldn't wait to say it. With wide eyes and a big, dimpled smile, she proclaimed, "My name is Emily Borodina, and I am from Ternopil!"

Gloria, a bit more subdued, followed suit, while I simply said that I was originally from northern Idaho, but Ternopil was home for our family. It was such a quick moment, yet it meant more than anyone in that room realized. We weren't displaced anymore. We had found a new home and a community that had embraced us and would continue to embrace us through the seasons to come.

In 2018 the new year dawned with great anticipation. We were preparing to break ground in the village where our home would be built. We hired an architect and gave her the daunting task of listening to the four of us dream about how we wanted our home to look. The girls, who had never experienced having rooms of their own, had some specific requests. Emily wanted a secret hiding place in her bedroom. Gloria wanted a reading nook and lots of bookshelves. My list was a bit longer. I wanted a pantry, a laundry room, an office, a walk-in closet in our bedroom, and a master bathroom with a tub looking out over the meadow. Ruslan wanted a detached garage and simply for his girls to be happy in their new house. We all wanted windows—lots of windows—so we could enjoy the view of our meadow and the forest beyond. We designed the house with people in mind. We wanted it to be a place where larger groups could come for fellowship.

Finally, in July, all the paperwork came through, and it was time to hire a building contractor. We were told we would have several to choose from, but that year the borders into Europe had opened for Ukrainians to travel and work without a visa. Much of the workforce had left to find higher paying jobs in the West. We found only one contractor available to build our house.

"Is it crazy to hire the only option available to build a house?" I asked Ruslan. "What if he is the most expensive or the least experienced builder?"

We finally decided that either the Lord would give us peace to hire this man or we would wait. We were already five months behind schedule, as the process of getting all the permits had taken longer than expected. Even if we hired a contractor now, we were pushing the clock to be able to finish the foundation, walls, and roof before winter set in.

The name of our prospective contractor was Rostislav. Ruslan met him at our attorney's office and then took him out to see the property. The man made a good impression, and Ruslan was eager for me to meet him. As we drove to another meeting at our attorney's office, I wondered what to ask. How could we determine if this man was honest or corrupt? How would we know if he loved building houses, or if it was just a job to pay the bills? We were praying for a man of integrity who had a passion for building. As I was introduced to Rostislav, a question popped into my head.

"Rostislav, what do you see when you look at the architectural plans for building our house?"

Without hesitation, he replied, "I really like the window designs and the way the house is positioned on the hill. You will have beautiful views."

It was a good answer, but I wanted to go deeper.

"Rostislav, do you know what I see when I look at these plans? I see my children finishing their childhoods. I see family and friends gathering for Christmas, Easter, and birthdays. I see my grandchildren coming home to visit us one day. If we decide to hire you, I want you to take seriously that we aren't just asking you to construct a building; we are asking you to build a home that we hope will serve our family for years to come."

I was the only woman in the room with Ruslan, our attorney, and the contractor. I knew what I was saying might sound overmuch, but in my mind, this man would be building the structure that our family would create a home in, and how he responded would speak loads about his character.

Rostislav looked me in the eye and replied, "I take seriously the fact that every house I build will become someone's home. That's why I recommend building safely and with quality materials. It would be my honor to build this home for you and your family."

Ruslan and I left the meeting, got back into our car, and agreed that we had found our contractor. After making a few more phone calls, we set the date for Rostislav and his crew to start building. Over the next month, we observed some amazing things. The first day on the job, Rostislav's team told us they had built our neighbor's home the year before. Our part of the village was mostly undeveloped with several houses in various stages of construction scattered across the countryside. Only three houses on our block were occupied. The crew building our house had met these neighbors, including one who owned a business that could rent us a backhoe, dump truck, cement truck, and almost everything else needed to build the foundation of our house. Thanks to these workers, Ruslan was introduced to all our neighbors.

We learned that every new neighborhood had a transformer that provided an allotted amount of electricity. If a neighborhood grew too large for one transformer, having a second transformer installed was costly and time consuming. Thankfully, our house received the last allotted kilowatts on the existing transformer.

Another thing I observed was that my husband was having the time of his life. He loved watching and directing the orchestra of daily events, often finding solutions to the inevitable challenges that arose. During warm fall days, the girls and I would pack a picnic and our favorite card game and watch the construction from a meadow next to our property. The girls giggled at the sight of their papa running around the worksite, directing the backhoe and dump truck. As we finished the second month of building, Rostislav told us that in fifteen years of building, he had never had a project move forward so smoothly. We were so thankful for God's favor.

In late September, YWAM Ternopil was involved in a multi-church worship event in the town square. There would be a harvest festival after the program, and our YWAM team helped organize several carnival-style booths. Ruslan and I arrived early to set up for the event, and as I looked out into the gathering early-morning crowd, I saw Rostislav.

Ruslan and I had wondered if our contractor was a believer. Now, here in the city square, we had an opportunity to ask.

"Good morning!" Ruslan said. "What are you doing here so bright and early?"

Rostislav flashed a smile. "Good morning to you too! It's good to see you! My church is participating in this morning's program, and I volunteered to help."

"Wow, that's wonderful," Ruslan said. "We are here doing the same thing! What church do you attend?"

"I attend Pastor Igor's church," Rostislav replied. "We meet in the Youth With A Mission building on Nova 2, if you know where that is."

Ruslan and I almost fell over—we were so shocked. We knew Pastor Igor well, and we of course knew that his church had been meeting in the basement of our building. To discover that this man we had met through professional channels was not only a believer but part of the church body that was meeting in our building was nothing short of a miracle. We told him of our connection with YWAM, and we all marveled at God's hand in orchestrating our relationship. We had been given only one choice for a contractor, and clearly, Rostislav was God's man for the job.

A few weeks later, it was time for our second trip back to Crimea. The purpose of this trip was to say our goodbyes and get our house ready to be sold, as we would need the funds to finish the new house. We packed for a two-week trip and made a quick stop to see Rostislav as we left town, since he wanted to talk about roofing for the new house. We met Rostislav alongside the road and spent a few minutes discussing our roofing options. Then he asked, "May I pray for you before you begin your journey?"

As I listened to Rostislav's beautiful prayer for safety on the roads and favor as we prepared our Simferopol house for sale, I felt overwhelmed by the goodness of God. The journey of closure to our life in Crimea was about to be completed. The decision to rebuild our life in Ternopil had not been an easy one, and yet from the moment we set out in faith along this new path, God continued to confirm that path in amazing ways. He was giving us an incredible story of coming home. And the stranger we had hired to build this new home was now the brother in Christ who was praying for God's blessing along this next part of our journey.

Excited to study history in our Ternopil homeschool program: Rebecca Taturevych with her students Elizabeth, Emily, Annabella, and Gloria

Digging the foundation for our house in Pidgorodne, Ukraine, one kilometer outside Ternopil city limits, 2018

CHAPTER 16

Farewell to Crimea

As we passed through the Russian border of occupied Crimea, I was aware of two things. The first was that Crimea didn't feel like home anymore. The second was gratitude for the gift of having closure. Coming back to our house in Simferopol was practical. We needed to box up, sell, or give away more of our possessions. We also needed to figure out what was needed to get the house on the market. These things were important—but for me, the luxury of this trip was in saying goodbye. I wanted our goodbyes to be a celebration, not a funeral.

I wanted to look at every corner of our home and yard and thank God for the memories we made there. I wanted a beautiful picture of the wall where we had marked the girls' heights as they grew. I wanted to spend time with our friends and thank God for all the years they were our community. I wanted the four of us to be able to look back on our eleven years in Simferopol and embrace the sweetness of this gift. And while there was sadness in saying goodbye, what we experienced throughout those last two weeks in Crimea was the freedom to be able to talk about our sweet memories in past tense. We were closing that chapter of our lives. It was finished. In some sense we could leave now, soaked in the significance of what this place had been to us.

Crimea was the first home where Ruslan and I put down roots. It's where we hammered out the foundation of our marriage and discovered we were going to be parents. It's where we brought our children home. They learned to crawl, walk, talk, and swim here on the Black Sea peninsula. Countless celebrations—Thanksgiving, harvest festivities, Easter, Christmas, the Fourth of July—took place here with missionaries who were like family, not just colleagues. Crimea is where we heard God speak to us about family ministry and where we began to live out our passion for helping equip families. Yes, God was repositioning us, but our history would go with us.

Two weeks later, with our minivan filled with as much as it could carry, we set off on the journey back to Ternopil. We had met with our real estate agent, Ivanna, and knew the steps we needed to take to sell the house. We still needed to get some paperwork in order, and there was furniture that would need to be sold, but our belongings were packed up and ready to be moved. Our plan was to return in the spring to finish emptying the house and then list it.

We once again had all our belongings searched at the Russian border crossing, then began our six-hundred-mile trip back to western Ukraine. Just a few miles into our westward travels, Ruslan and I looked at each other and commented on the overwhelming sense that we were going home. It was that feeling after being gone on a long trip, and suddenly you are just ready to be in your own neighborhood, in your own space, sleeping in your own bed. We marveled at this, because it had been almost five years since we had experienced this emotion. Home was in a new direction, and we were heading there!

Later that fall, after Thanksgiving, I flew home to spend ten days with my mom. Mom was doing well adapting to life as a widow, but she needed a lot of support. I wanted to spend some time with her just to see how she was doing and to bring a little joy to her holiday season.

About five days into my trip, Ruslan called me. "Sharyn," he said, "you aren't going to believe this. Ivanna just called. Even though we had agreed not to list the house until spring, she went ahead and listed it anyway. She was sure there wouldn't be any buyers at the price we were asking but was curious to see what kind of interest it might generate. It wasn't even listed for twenty-four hours, and she has a buyer, at full price, ready to go as soon as possible."

"Wow, that's amazing. What needs to happen?"

"We need your signature on some documents to start the process of selling the house. As soon as you get back here and sign those documents, I'll need to leave for Simferopol."

This was crazy news on many levels. We had friends who had been trying to sell their much newer homes in Simferopol for almost two years without success. The Russian invasion hadn't exactly helped the real-estate market. How was it possible that we had a buyer, at our full asking price, not even twenty-four hours after the house was listed? It had to be God, and we had to work fast.

Five days later, I flew back to Ukraine and signed the paperwork, and the next day Ruslan left for the two-day trip back to Simferopol. As usual, we were in uncharted territory. There isn't exactly a how-to manual for selling your house in an area now controlled by Russian occupiers. Ruslan would have about twelve days to prepare the documents, sell our furniture, rent a storage unit for our remaining boxes, and find a way to get the money from the sale out of Crimea. Because of the sanctions imposed on Russia, the banking system didn't work outside the Russian Federation. The sale would be done in hard cash (US dollars), and Ruslan would then have to figure out how to move the cash to Ukraine.

The first five days of his trip were a whirlwind, but Ruslan was able to get the house cleared out and make it through most of his checklist. The next day, December 20, he would sign the house over to the new owners. That left just enough time for him to get home to celebrate Christmas in Ternopil.

Before Ruslan could sell the house, he needed one last document. He had to go to the utilities office and get a document saying that all the utilities had been paid in full. It was a simple process, so he and Ivanna had waited until the last minute to get it done. As they approached the building, a security guard stopped them and explained that they needed to get a ticket for their appointment time. Ruslan walked up to the ticket machine, pressed the button, and was shocked to see his appointment wouldn't be for seven business days. Hopeful for some kind of exception, Ruslan walked up to the window to plead with the attendant.

"Ticket please," the woman said.

Ruslan handed her the ticket.

"Your appointment isn't for another seven days."

"I am so sorry, but I didn't realize there was such a long waiting period. I am selling my house tomorrow, and I need the document that shows I don't owe anything for utilities."

The woman scowled. "Don't you see that the people whose appointments are for this time are already coming to the window?" She motioned for Ruslan to go and left no space for further conversation.

Ruslan sat down by Ivanna and began to think through the situation. To wait seven business days in Crimea meant that he would miss Christmas with us. If he went home for Christmas and then returned, it meant having to drive the twelve-hundred-mile round trip a second time. Tensions between Russia and Ukraine continued so there was also the risk that the borders could close at any time. There didn't seem to be any good option.

Feeling incredibly frustrated, Ruslan began to pray. *God, I'm not sure what I should do.*

A few moments passed. Then Ruslan saw that the man who had gone up to the window after him was beckoning Ruslan to join him.

Great, Ruslan thought. *He's probably going to scold me for talking to the lady during his appointment time.* With some trepidation, he walked up to the man and said hello.

"Don't you have a ticket for today?" the man asked.

"No, I don't," Ruslan replied.

The man pulled a ticket out of his coat pocket. "I was here a week ago, and I took two tickets. I've just used the first one, and this one is scheduled for twenty minutes from now." As if it had been his plan all along, he handed the ticket to Ruslan, turned around, and left.

Twenty minutes later, speechless with gratitude, Ruslan walked out of the building with the needed document. When he called me that evening to tell me what had happened, his voice was full of emotion. Why had that man taken two tickets a week earlier? What were the chances that he would have been in the building with both tickets—and close enough to overhear Ruslan explaining his predicament to the clerk? And why would he care enough to offer his other ticket to a stranger? As far as Ruslan was concerned, that man was an angel, and the provision of that ticket a miracle from heaven.

The following day, Ruslan and Ivanna went to the office of the attorney who was brokering the sale. Both parties arrived with all the required documentation, and everything was reviewed and double checked. Ruslan then asked when it would be time for him to sign the deed and for the buyers to hand over the money. Immediately, everyone stood up and left the room except for the real estate agents, the buyer, and Ruslan, presumably to allow some privacy for counting all the money.

Ruslan then realized he hadn't brought anything to carry the cash. When he sheepishly explained his problem to one of the attorneys, the man handed him a plastic grocery bag. Ruslan felt a little funny carrying a grocery bag full of cash to the bank next door, but it served the purpose just fine. Ivanna had arranged to rent a safe-deposit box in which to store the money until we could figure out how best to get it to Ternopil.

At the time, an individual was allowed to bring only ten thousand dollars out of Crimea without having to pay large custom taxes. After much discussion, Ruslan decided to leave for the border with three of our good friends from Simferopol. Each person would carry ten thousand dollars over the border for us. The rest of the funds would have to stay in the safe-deposit box until we could find a way to get it out.

I didn't like that Ruslan would have so much cash on him as he traveled alone through Ukraine, but after weeks of unsuccessful effort to find a way to get money out of Crimea through a wire transfer, the best we could do was to literally walk it across the border! This was crazy. But so was the whole story of selling our house and saying goodbye to Crimea.

Now we were starting a new era of our family ministry, and we knew it was a miracle of God's provision from start to finish. We decided we would use half of the sale proceeds to finish our new home and the other half for developing the Carpathian retreat cabin. What a story God was giving us!

Front view of our home of eight years on Barisheva Street, Simferopol, Ukraine

Our home looking toward the house from the backyard

CHAPTER 17

The Valley and the Mountaintop

As our house progressed during the new year, 2019, we loved visiting on the weekends. It was always amazing to see how much had been accomplished in a week's time. I loved our little village, and with every trip I marveled that this was where we would get to live.

My dream has always been to live in the country on a ranch or farm, with horses, chickens, honeybee hives, and a big vegetable garden. Pidgorodne, our soon-to-be village home, felt like a country getaway even though it was just a half mile outside Ternopil city limits. We could see chickens, turkeys, ducks, goats, cows, horses, kittens, and puppies every which way we looked.

We soon discovered that a host of wild animals were also our neighbors. Foxes, wild hares, and broods of partridges hid in the tall grass outside our house. In the spring, storks and herons flew back from their winter retreats to fish for frogs in the stream that winds through our meadow. We also noticed owls perched on light poles near our garage, and it was fascinating to watch them hunt rodents in the tall grass.

Although Pidgorodne is one of the older villages outside Ternopil, our neighborhood was virtually new. We could spend hours just wandering along the little roads and paths that circled the town's garden plots and farms. We took every opportunity to meet our neighbors, and we hoped to be moved in by the end of 2019.

But in March, I got called back to the States to help my mom. It had been five years since her dementia diagnosis, and we had new concerns that she was failing fast mentally. I needed to assess whether she could continue living at home by herself.

Mom was so social that when you talked with her on the phone or dropped by for a quick visit, she appeared to be just a delightful older woman with some memory problems. However, the story I had heard from her caregiver and from a longtime friend was that Mom's condition was reaching a point where it might not be safe for her to live alone any longer.

Even after spending time with Mom myself, I still didn't know how to make a decision like this. One day Mom seemed great, and I thought she could make it through another year with just the support of caregivers checking in daily. Then there were days when Mom fed the dog ten times in twenty-four hours because every time she dozed off or took a nap, she woke up and thought it was morning. As a result, her dog, Sara, looked more like a hippopotamus than a black Lab.

If Mom were to move, the best option available was a charming assisted-living community an hour from Priest Lake. To move meant she would have to leave her home of more than thirty years as well her dog and one of her cats. She would leave everything that was normal and familiar. It broke my heart to even think about this. Worse, there was no way to prepare Mom for the move. I would talk to her about the idea and we would agree that it was for the best, but two hours later she would have forgotten everything we discussed.

I agonized through May, June, and July about what to do. I couldn't sleep at night. I knew that somehow God was going to work it all out, but I couldn't convince myself to stop stressing over making the decision. Even though this decision was significant, I was troubled by the amount of internal turmoil the situation was causing in me. I was at a loss for what course of action would be best. Finally, I decided we would keep Mom home for another year—unless something happened to convince me, beyond a shadow of a doubt, that it was time to move her.

Ruslan, the girls, and I had been blessed with the opportunity to stay in our church's parsonage that spring and summer, just ten miles from my mom's house. Since our stay was longer than usual, it was wonderful to have our own space. We visited churches in our region, and the girls attended school, but we could easily drop in throughout the week to see my mom.

In late August I drove over one Sunday morning to pick up Mom for church. As I arrived, I saw Mom wandering around outside looking confused and distressed. When she saw me, she said the door to the house wasn't working. "It's broken," she kept saying.

Mom had locked herself out of the house and misplaced the hidden outside key. Instead of going to the neighbors for help, she had spent the night cold and uncomfortable in the backseat of the car in the garage.

That incident was the confirmation I needed to make the impossible decision. We decided to move in with Mom for the rest of August and September to help care for her until arrangements could be completed for her to move into The Bridge, an assisted-living community in Sandpoint.

For reasons I didn't understand, the process of moving my mother felt more painful for me than everything we had experienced coming out of Crimea and even my dad's passing away. I could feel myself falling apart. I was grieving having to give the dog and one of Mom's cats away. They both were precious to Mom and all of us. Separating them felt so cruel. I grieved that with Mom's move, we were closing out almost forty years of the Magers family living at this address. Most of all, I grieved the heartbreak I knew Mom would experience.

The Lord had assured me many times that summer of his care for my mom. He would show the way forward, and my job was to simply trust and obey. Yet I remained in such distress.

We moved my mom on a beautiful fall day in late September. I explained to her that it was moving day. We packed just a few things: the remaining cat in its carrier and a few articles of clothing. I had spent the previous week furnishing and decorating Mom's apartment with familiar mementos from home. On our way, we stopped by the one-hundred-year-old Newport Cemetery, where my dad is buried. We left flowers at his grave and talked about how he would want Mom to be well cared for and safe. We arrived at The Bridge in time for dinner and enjoyed meeting all the nice people. For the next couple days, I did the best I could to help Mom settle into her new living arrangements.

The transition was much easier than I expected. Mom trusted me so much that she allowed me to lead her into this community. When she started to worry and feel afraid, she believed me when I told her that everything was okay, that I loved her, and that most important, Jesus loved her. It was a hard time, but Mom persevered through it and found a lot of joy in making new friends and participating in The Bridge's daily activities.

By mid-October, we had secured Mom's house so that it could sit through the winter uninhabited, and we felt Mom was settled enough that we could go home to Ukraine. Honestly, I couldn't wait to leave. We had done what needed to be done in those six months, but it had cost me a lot emotionally, and I was ready for some time to recover.

One of the joys of going home to Ukraine was seeing our new house again. It had been transformed since we last saw it in March. The focus now was on the inside, and I eagerly dived into the project. We made countless trips to home improvement stores to pick out tiles, fixtures, sinks, bathtubs, and vanities. Then just before Thanksgiving, in a tile and bath shop called Vero, I noticed something odd. Ruslan and I were there to pick out a tile pattern, and I could not decide which to choose. I literally could not get my brain to say, "Let's go with that one." Unlike the decisions I had made for my mother, the choice before me was not important. Yet I was paralyzed. On another occasion, while choosing toilets for our bathrooms, I felt a huge wave of anxiety rush over me. This was followed by uncontrollable tears. Why was something as simple as picking out toilets causing an emotional meltdown?

Later, on a day trip to the nearby city of Lviv, I noticed that every time Ruslan passed a car or even needed to maneuver just a little bit, I experienced a jolt of adrenaline. Every time a worrisome thought entered my mind, adrenaline surged through my body. As I looked ahead at all we needed to accomplish over the next six months—homeschool for the girls, the countless decisions that needed to be made to finish our house, moving, and ministry—I felt overwhelmed and depressed. I didn't feel like smiling anymore. I didn't want to get out of bed in the morning. I didn't want to be around people. I felt as if something inside me had broken, but I had no idea what it was or how to fix it.

In late January 2020, I decided to go to Le Rucher, a debriefing ministry in France just outside Geneva, Switzerland. I hoped that processing the events of the past year with trained professionals might help me fix whatever was wrong. The five days I spent in France were restful and beautiful. Mont Blanc loomed white overhead, and in between sessions I walked through the nearby French villages and just prayed and processed. By the end of the debriefing, I was diagnosed with mid-stage burnout. In burnout, people experience physical, mental, and emotional exhaustion as a result of long-term stress. The Le Rucher staff explained to me that if I didn't take time to heal, the burnout could have significant consequences for my health.

When you break a leg or an arm, the doctor prescribes treatment and time to heal. As I was discovering, it was the same with a broken heart. Over the past several years, we had gone through political upheaval, displacement, death in our family, the house construction, and now my mom's move. I had finally hit that proverbial wall. I needed time to walk through and process the impact of what I had experienced. I needed time to convince my adrenal system that I wasn't in crisis anymore.

I returned to Ukraine very relieved that I wasn't losing my mind. What ailed me had a name—and a cure. The next question was how to walk out the healing process.

Our lives were as busy and crazy as always. The girls were working hard in school; Ruslan was still working on the house; and we were planning and coordinating events. We decided to attend conferences in Prague and Budapest, but I felt like I was just limping along. On the outside, I looked normal; I could function and get the job done. But on the inside, I felt numb and lifeless.

"Just smile, Mom, even if you don't feel like it," Emily said one morning. I am normally a happy person, and it made me sad that I didn't feel like smiling. But it also blessed me that my family was prodding me to exercise those smile muscles until they worked again on their own.

I began to meet weekly with a wonderful friend and spiritual director named Issie Smith. Her friendship and coaching helped me slowly move forward—and to look back. I also formed a grief-share group with some of the women from the YWAM base. As I studied burnout and looked more closely at what happens to a person physically when under prolonged stress,

I was amazed at the chemistry of the body and the coping mechanisms God created in us so that we could walk through great difficulty and challenges.

I prayed that with the first blossoms of spring, maybe new life would spring up in me. I prayed that as God was repositioning us into our new house, he would reposition me spiritually with a season of rest.

Something new was coming. When I closed my eyes, I could almost see the mountaintop up ahead. As people prayed for us, many of their Spirit-filled words hinted at new vision and new platforms of influence. We felt the Lord saying that 2020 would be a sabbatical year for us. We resolved to engage in that sabbatical year as best we could. It was a timely word, because soon the whole world would be taking a sabbatical, whether they wanted to or not.

In March, the Covid pandemic hit, and as it did in the rest of the world, life in Ukraine came to a screeching halt. Airports shut down. Restaurants closed. Schools tried to figure out how to go online. Most people worked from home or didn't work at all.

As crazy as it sounds, for me it was a miracle. It cleared my ministry schedule indefinitely and moved all our base and other ministry meetings to Zoom. It allowed our family to focus on finishing our house, finishing the girls' school year, and packing, which was plenty of work in itself. It also created space for me to focus on things that brought me life, and one of the most life-giving aspects of this season was agreeing with a small group of friends to socially isolate together. Our base leaders, Lance and Megan Roberts, and their son, Beniah, plus new YWAM Ternopil staffer Wanda Taft, became our in-person community during the months of isolation. Almost every week, we would drive into the countryside and explore the ruins of castles, monasteries, and abandoned cathedrals. We walked for miles through the fields and forests near our house and did our best to keep the prescribed distance from one another.

As March turned into April and April into May, I began to feel like my old self again.

CHAPTER 18

Harvest

The pandemic wasn't the only big change to hit YWAM Ternopil. Lance and Megan, who led our base for nearly six years, decided to transition out of leadership. These two wonderful servant leaders had taught us so much about shepherding and discipleship. They had accomplished much and were loved by so many, but they were tired. We knew they needed rest and time to pray about the next season of their ministry.

The base assembled a search team to look for, prayerfully consider, and recruit their replacements. The team included individuals from other bases in Ukraine as well as our European leader, Dick Brouwer. I was asked to represent the staff of YWAM Ternopil on the search team. It was a great group, and I looked forward to working together on this important decision.

My job was to give feedback about staff perspectives. We invited our staff to submit names of individuals they thought would be good candidates. Ruslan and I spent many hours discussing whom we might nominate.

Prior to our next search-team meeting, a list of nominated candidates was compiled and emailed to those of us on the team. When I opened the email and began scanning the names, I nearly fell off my chair. My name was on the list. What? Ruslan and I hadn't even considered ourselves possible candidates. Due to one family crisis after another, we kept getting yanked to the other side of the Atlantic Ocean. Each time I felt terrible about having to push the pause button on our responsibilities in Ternopil. I was flattered that someone had faith that our situation would finally stabilize and we could be trusted with the responsibility of leading the base. After my heart rate returned to normal, Ruslan and I decided that any of the candidates could be great. We would wait and see what happened after the next team meeting.

A few days later, the team gathered on Zoom to go over the names. We talked through the pluses and minuses of the various people who had been suggested. When my name came up, I chuckled and said I was quite surprised to see myself on the list.

Feeling a bit awkward, I said simply, "I'm sure we will find someone better suited for the job."

When we came to the end of the list, one person asked if anyone had other thoughts about candidates, pointing out that the new base leadership could be a single individual or a combination of people.

Anya Schlegel, co-director of YWAM Kyiv, said, "Actually, of all the names on this list, I like the idea of Ruslan and Sharyn as potential candidates. I was so happy to see your name, Sharyn, because I have thought for some time now that you and Ruslan could do a great job."

Others in the group agreed with Anya's statement. Someone also suggested considering one of our up-and-coming leaders on the base, Yaroslav Yagotin, who was a gifted evangelist and apostolic leader. Dick Brouwer liked the idea of considering a shared leadership platform, in which Ruslan, Yaroslav, and I would split the responsibilities of leading the base. Everyone agreed that this was an interesting idea and thought our giftings could work well together.

As I listened to all the different thoughts and ideas being shared in this discussion, I felt like I was having an out-of-body experience. I had an ongoing conversation with God in my head, even as the team was thinking through all the possibilities.

Lord, are they really talking about us? What if they ask us to consider this? Is this a good idea? Is this your idea? God, this whole idea is so incredibly crazy and unexpected that it makes me feel like your fingerprints are all over it.

As I got to the end of my impromptu conversation with God, I realized that everyone was looking at me—as much as you can look at someone via a Zoom conference.

"Sharyn, would you and Ruslan be open to us taking a closer look at the two of you, together with Yaroslav, as potential candidates for base leadership?"

I took a deep breath, exhaled, and said Ruslan and I would discuss it and pray about it and get back to them.

That weekend, Ruslan and I took a long walk through the forest near our soon-to-be-completed house. We had been discussing for days the possibility of leading the second largest base in Ukraine into a new season of ministry. We had talked things over with Lance and Megan and, of course, with Yaroslav, whom we affectionately called Senya for short. Those conversations were encouraging, positive, and even exciting. As Ruslan and I prayed and talked together, we felt strongly that whether we said yes or no to this potential opportunity, we were moving into something new. A chapter was about to turn, and we were excited to see what it would look like.

We realized there was still something inside us from all those years ago when Lance had so aptly called us base leaders in waiting. What if the waiting had led us to this opportunity to lead this base and its incredible community of missionaries? We loved the idea of coming alongside the staff to support them and help them be even more effective in the work they were doing. We foresaw new doors opening for our teams, schools, and ministries. It was exciting to think about being part of the National Leadership Team, which is made up of base and national ministry leaders.

After talking with several close friends back in the States, and to the girls, we believed that the invitation—and especially the timing of it, the unexpectedness of it—had all the earmarks of a God-originated idea. We felt peace to say yes, we were open to being considered. The next step would be an interview with the transition team. If the team decided to recommend us together with Senya, then the staff of YWAM Ternopil would be invited to share their thoughts and feelings about the team's recommendation. The process wasn't expected to take more than a few weeks.

In the meantime, on May 29 we celebrated Gloria's fifteenth birthday at our new house. We weren't living there yet, but the house was finished enough to host a fun day for our beloved daughter. Gloria's birthday felt like the official opening of the Borodin family residence. We kept the gathering small, as Ukraine officially was still shut down due to Covid. However, in our area, people were slowly coming together again. Ternopil residents found ways to keep their businesses going, and they were both practical and careful in their daily lives. They couldn't afford to sit at home without a paycheck indefinitely. That was just the reality.

The week after Gloria's birthday, all our bedrooms were painted. The built-in closets arrived and were assembled, and we purchased mattresses and beds and assembled those as well. We slowly began bringing things into our new house. We had very little furniture to move, so that part wasn't hard, but sorting through and packing the odds and ends of life was grueling. On June 5, we decided that the house was done enough for us to start sleeping there. Ruslan spent the next day clearing the way for our first night, while the girls and I cleaned out the kitchen, bathroom, and closets at our townhouse apartment. We collected our dog, Mimi, and the girls' fish and aquariums, and we were ready for our new home.

With an energy and excitement that was different from anything we had felt before, the girls and I stepped out of the little townhouse we had lived in for six years, packed up our red mini-car, and around six in the evening headed home. *Home. Our home.* Oh, what a privilege to have one again.

Our drive was quiet, thoughtful, as if we were holding our breath, waiting to exhale. As I turned off the highway and made the turn under the Pidgorodne portal that June evening, I felt like we were crossing a threshold into our future.

That evening as we unloaded our car and began unpacking our things into our new bedrooms, I felt such joy. We had come full circle—we were home again. A home full of life, love, and laughter. We would get to watch our girls finish growing up in this house. We would get to open the doors to our friends and family and to our new neighbors. Gratitude poured out from within me. Being uprooted had been so hard; being replanted in this new community felt like such an incredible gift. Our journey led us to the top of the mountain. The view was more beautiful than I could have imagined.

Ruslan and I woke up the next morning, poured ourselves some coffee, and went outside onto our deck to watch the early morning sunshine awaken the meadows below us. The cacophony of bird song, quiet breeze, and grazing animals was intoxicating. It was a morning clear and crisp. Everything glistened and sparkled. As I looked out at the beauty all around us, I realized that one chapter of our journey had ended, and we could see ahead again, literally as well as figuratively. God had given us a house on a hill, and we could see for miles in almost every direction. We were no longer walking through the thicket.

I went into my brand-new kitchen and began to prepare breakfast for the first time. We sat around the table in our kitchen nook and talked about what it was like sleeping in our bedrooms for the first night. After breakfast, I looked at my phone and saw there was a message from the leadership transition team. I opened it and read the official invitation for Ruslan and me to become the co-directors of YWAM Ternopil in a shared leadership platform with Senya.

Once again, we all marveled at the timing. Wasn't it just like God to orchestrate the official invitation of such a significant move in our ministry to coincide with the deep meaning of this move into a new home?

I never would have thought that I could look back on seven years of such challenges and feel such gratitude. I never would have thought God could turn my heartbreak into a heart full of thankfulness for all the beautiful things that came through the difficulties. He brought new life out of the ashes. He used the hardest things to grow in us a faith and trust in him that was unlike anything we had known before.

The Bible teaches that God draws close to the brokenhearted, and I realized that in that space, we experienced his presence in a powerful way. We survived those hard times because we held on to Jesus with all that was in us. And in that closeness, his presence changed us. God made us stronger. In our weakest moments, he cultivated in us new compassion, resilience, tenacity, and grit. Little did we know that the journey wasn't yet finished—we would need every ounce of those qualities to face what was coming next.

Home sweet home, our home in the village of Pidgorodne

Commissioning day as leaders of YWAM Ternopil, 2020
Left to right: Oksana and Andrew Ford, our Ukraine national leaders; Yaroslav and Oksana Yagotin, our YWAM Ternopil co-leaders; Sharyn and Ruslan; Lance and Megan Roberts, outgoing YWAM Ternopil leaders

CHAPTER 19

New Storm Clouds over Ukraine

As 2021 began, our YWAM base was booming. Our team of missionaries were doing new things in new ways and seeing some great results! We loved being part of the new base leadership team and soon began figuring out how to steer the YWAM Ternopil ship, so to speak.

One of the most exciting parts of that year was hosting short-term teams from Montana, Hawaii, Idaho, Germany, and Kyiv. Working with outreach teams has always been one of my favorite ministries. I love coming alongside young people, on their first adventure in missions, and helping them learn to love and understand Ukraine. I try to help them build a foundation for missions that I hope will stay with them for the rest of their lives. We invited many of these teams into our new home that year, to hear their stories and to share ours, and to encourage them as they stepped out in faith.

One new ministry our base launched that year was a youth outreach called PidWall. The name means basement in Ukrainian, and our youth meetings were indeed held in the basement of our YWAM building. It was a place for the unchurched to come and be inspired by young people who were living for Jesus. They would play games, perform lively music sets, and often share testimonies of how choosing a relationship with God had saved them from a life of self-destruction. They talked of what it meant to have a purpose and identity in Christ. It was beautiful to see many kids from our neighborhood give their lives to Jesus.

Our base was also engaged in pioneering works toward feeding the homeless, visiting orphanages, assisting rehab ministry programs, planting churches in area villages, and continuing the development of Metamorphosis, our K–12 Christian school, the very first Christian educational establishment in our city.

As the fall of 2021 approached, Roma and Rebecca were leading a team about to pioneer the first Biblical Core Course offered in both Ukrainian and English. This University of the Nations secondary school teaches people how to effectively study the Bible using the inductive Bible study method. We hoped that this school would inspire people to be passionate about studying the Bible and living by its principles. Our little mission base was thriving, and we were loving the joy of watching YWAM Ternopil's family of ministries reach the lost with God's love.

In November I began getting strange emails from friends and family back in the States. They asked if we were doing okay, what with Russia mobilizing soldiers along the Russia-Ukraine border. I didn't think much about it because Russia was always doing something along our border. Since I hadn't heard a single conversation of concern among any of our friends and colleagues in Ternopil, or from my husband, I figured these emails just meant the US press was stirring things up again.

By mid-December those emails were coming in more frequently, and I decided it might be prudent to ask Ruslan if there was something going on that I should be concerned about.

"Honey, I keep getting these concerning messages from friends in the States," I said. "Is there something happening on the border with Russia?"

"Actually, there is a lot of concern about the situation on the border right now," Ruslan replied. "More soldiers have been mobilized for what Russia calls military exercises than have ever been seen before. There's a lot of worry that it could mean an escalation in the war."

"Okay, so how worried should I be?" I asked

"I think we have to take this seriously and be ready for anything," Ruslan answered.

That was not the response I was looking for. I couldn't imagine Putin doing something as crazy as launching a full-scale invasion of Ukraine. Putin and his government were many things, but they weren't idiots. In my mind, attacking a country of forty million people situated next door to the European Union would be a disastrous move for the Russian Federation.

Since most Ukrainians didn't seem worried, I decided not to worry either. I knew Ruslan would tell me if things got worse. Full-scale war was inconceivable. Ridiculous. Wasn't it?

We started 2022 with two Discipleship Training School outreach teams, one from Montana and one from Maui, serving through our base. Before their arrival, I had met via Zoom with the school leaders back in the USA, and they had both asked for a written evacuation protocol in the event of a Russian invasion. I was a tad annoyed by the request because I still didn't believe such an invasion would occur. But I recognized that the parents of the DTS students were worried by what they were watching on the news. As our leadership team began to discuss what our evacuation protocols might be, almost everyone continued to believe that nothing was going to happen.

The general consensus was that there just wasn't any way that Russia was going to start a full-scale war with Ukraine. But if something happened, our evacuation protocol was simple. The airport was just two hours away, and the borders were also close if we needed to drive people out.

Ruslan, however, had a different perspective.

"If Russia invades," Ruslan began, "all the airports will be shut down. Flying out will not be an option. If a full-scale war breaks out, there will be millions of people trying to escape over the borders. It will be next to impossible to get out that way. And lastly, if Russia attacks, the entire country will be placed under martial law, and Ukrainian men will not be able to cross the border. I expect there will be strict curfews as well. My feeling is that we need to come up with a plan of evacuation for these teams that would be initiated ahead of a full-scale attack."

The room fell silent as we all began to think through the ramifications of what Ruslan had said. Even though we still didn't think it would happen, we began to realize that as leaders we had to prepare for the worst-case scenario.

We wrote up an evacuation plan that would be required for any visiting teams and recommended for staff living in Ternopil. If fighting broke out in any new areas of Ukraine, our teams would evacuate. If embassies began evacuating their staff, our teams would evacuate. We had drawn the line, and we hoped to God it wouldn't be crossed.

For me, I think that was the beginning of that familiar sick feeling in my gut, the feeling that accompanies the realization that things might be more serious than anyone wanted to consider. I couldn't ignore all the headlines anymore. The value of the Ukrainian hryvnia was falling, and foreign embassies were talking about closing. World leaders were convening. Russia hadn't sent one soldier across the border, yet it had thrown Ukraine into a state of upheaval.

I spent hours on the phone every day talking to ministry partners, journalists, and radio talk shows, as well as our own friends and family, trying to help them understand what we were experiencing inside Ukraine. I did my best to answer their questions, talk through our evacuation policies, and process whether teams should come or not, stay or not. I always shared prayer points for our base and for Ukraine, especially that the leaders of the world would have wisdom to deescalate the present crisis. The strange thing was, it still felt like people in the US and Western Europe were far more concerned about the situation here than the Ukrainian people were themselves.

On January 20, rumors began to fly across the media that the United States embassy was evacuating nonessential workers. I was on a mother-daughter getaway weekend with Gloria in Lviv, when Jeremy West, the DTS director at YWAM Montana, called to find out what we were hearing in Ukraine. He was concerned that the line was being crossed and that we needed to think about evacuating the Montana team we were hosting. As we talked about this recent news, I looked on the embassy website and found nothing about evacuations listed there. I had an emergency contact number at the US embassy in Kyiv. I called and was reassured that there was no such protocol in effect. I hung up, texted Jeremy what I had learned, and chalked it up as fake news.

Unfortunately, two days later, a front-page story said the US embassy was indeed evacuating nonessential personnel over the next two weeks. I was frustrated that my contact at the embassy hadn't told me the truth just forty-eight hours earlier. We soon learned that the order was prompted by

US intelligence indicating an attack was coming. My brain was still having a hard time connecting all these details. It seemed odd that the US government was acting with so little urgency in its evacuation if officials really believed a major escalation was coming. If a full-scale attack was imminent, why take two weeks to pack up and leave? Whatever the case, one of our emergency protocol lines had been crossed, and now we had to act.

As it turns out, it wasn't easy to get entire teams of people over the borders quickly—not because it wasn't easy to get to a border, but because we were still under Covid restrictions. Everyone had to have a negative Covid test within twenty-four hours of crossing the border. Try getting multiple negative Covid test results, then booking tickets out on a plane, bus, or train in such a time frame! It was very difficult! We discovered that once we had the Covid test results in hand the best option was just to drive our teams to the borders, where they could then walk across. Ruslan and Senya began to joke about who was making the most middle-of-the-night runs to the Polish or Romanian borders in our YWAM bus. Those Covid test results invariably arrived late evening, which meant traveling late into the night.

During that late January and early February, we evacuated three teams, with a total of twenty-nine students. I was so sorry these students' outreaches ended this way, but I could understand why their parents would want to move them to a safer place. Ruslan and I now started and finished our days watching the news reports. US President Joe Biden kept saying that Russia was going to attack. He would even predict when it was going to happen. I kept thinking how bizarre that was. I'm no war expert, but it seemed outrageous that Putin would announce when he would launch an invasion! We thought that whatever days were advertised were probably not the ones we had to worry about.

By this point, the level of alertness and concern my husband was communicating was reminiscent of the days prior to the invasion of Crimea. He had begun suggesting that the girls and I leave the country. It was not an idea that our teenage daughters or I wanted to think about even for a minute. We had gone through one evacuation, and we had no desire to do that again. Besides that, I was now one of the base leaders. What kind of example would it set if I evacuated? We continued in our holding pattern, but Ruslan asked us to be ready, to have our bags packed, because things were not looking good.

We held a meeting with all our YWAM Ternopil staff and encouraged them to follow our cautious lead. Of course, we were all praying that Russia would not attack, but now we all considered it a possibility. We told the staff to have their exit plan ready and to prepare a go bag with documents, water, energy bars, cell phone battery packs, and valuables that they could grab quickly. We talked about whom to call if they were going to leave, so we would know who was staying and who was going. For many on our base, it was the first time they were forced to truly consider the significance of what could happen.

On February 10, Ruslan made the decision that the girls and I would leave the country. "I do not feel like it is a safe situation for you to stay any longer," he said. "Take a vacation. Go visit your mom. But I just need you to leave the country for a couple of weeks. Just in case."

We were just weeks away from the eighth anniversary of the Crimea invasion. How could it be that we were having these same conversations again? I was so angry. The girls were angry too. We did not want to leave. We had loved every moment of living in our home over the past year and a half. Already countless gatherings had been hosted there—sleepovers with the girls' friends and fellowship nights with Ternopil staff and teams. We were planning to plant a garden that spring and open the yard for outdoor barbecues. We were fully engaged in our community and did not want a disruption.

Lord, please, I prayed, *I want to honor my husband. I trust him, and I know he is making this decision because he wants us to be safe. But we don't desire to go, Lord. Please, bring confirmation to all of us if you want us to leave. With all that is within me, I don't want to leave my husband, our home, and this community, especially if further trouble is coming.*

Within hours of that prayer, I received a call from the States that there was a situation with my mother that needed to be addressed at our earliest convenience. My mom was still living in the assisted-living community. She was doing as well as could be expected considering her dementia and the Covid restrictions. Other concerns had come to my attention over the past few months, but I had hoped they would keep until our scheduled trip to Idaho in the summer. We decided that this latest phone call was the confirmation we had asked for. Mom needed us; that was reason enough to make an unscheduled trip.

The girls and I began preparing to leave Ukraine in the next forty-eight hours. We would travel eight hours by train to Kraków, Poland, on February 15. We chose Kraków even though the Lviv airport was much closer, because if fighting broke out into all of Ukraine, commercial airports would be closed. I didn't yet have our plane tickets, but we decided I could work on getting them after we got into Kraków.

If Ruslan had his way, we would have already left, but I had a small Valentine's Day event planned for our staff, and I wanted to follow through with it. I also insisted that I needed at least forty-eight hours to emotionally and physically prepare to go. It wasn't only about packing our suitcases; I also had to prepare our homeschool program to be on the road for two to three weeks, and that always took time. I needed time to clean the house, wrap up a few things at work, and say a quick goodbye to our friends.

On Tuesday February13, I found myself at home with time to pack. But instead of reaching for our suitcases, I cranked up the worship music in the living room, and I headed to the basement to find my box of spring and Easter decorations. When the house was sufficiently decorated, I began to clean it. To deep clean. I washed cupboards, dusted baseboards, and put items in their respective places. I tackled my laundry pile, making sure there were plenty of fresh sheets and linens, just in case we might have company while we were away. Even though there were a thousand other things I needed to do, getting my house ready felt exceedingly important. I was making a statement that I was leaving on my terms. I was doing something normal, something enjoyable for the spring and Easter season as I did every year. I wasn't evacuating. We were going to visit my mom and find out how to fix her situation. I would be back in just a couple weeks. But in the back of my mind, just in case, I wanted my home to be ready, as I would want it to be, to embrace what might be coming. I wanted that picture in my mind of my home neat and tidy, decorated for spring, just in case.

I couldn't bear to think it—just in case I never got to come home again.

War is coming. A man embraces the cross, February 24, 2022, Lviv, Ukraine, the first day of full-scale war.
Photo Credit: Dennis Melnichuk

CHAPTER 20

When War Comes Home

We landed in Spokane on February 22, 2022, and twenty-four hours later, Russia launched a full-scale military invasion of Ukraine.

The news broke around seven thirty in the evening, Pacific time. The girls and I were exhausted from our travels and the ten-hour time difference, but we decided to stay awake a little longer to watch ABC's nightly news report. It was early morning in Ukraine. People were still in bed or just beginning to start their day. Suddenly a news flash appeared, saying we were going live to Lviv, Ukraine, where Martha Raddatz, ABC's Chief Global Affairs Correspondent, was covering a breaking news story.

It was a surreal moment for Gloria, Emily, and me. The seasoned reporter seemed almost apologetic as she uttered the words we'd been so sure the world would never hear.

"Russia has attacked. I repeat, Russia is attacking Ukraine as I speak. We have confirmed reports that bombs are exploding around Kyiv and other cities. As the people of Ukraine wake up this morning, their worst fears have come true."

My mind went quiet. It was almost like I couldn't hear what the reporter was saying. I thought she must be mistaken. My mind simply could not grasp the reality of what was unfolding.

"Mom! Call Papa!" The voices of my children broke me free from shock. I jumped off the couch and made the call, waking my husband at 5:30 a.m. I told him what we had seen on TV news, and he hung up to see what the Ukrainian news channels were reporting. The next thing I did was get on Facebook to see if any of our friends in Ukraine were posting. As I read the posts, I couldn't believe my eyes. Friend after friend, colleague after colleague, reported explosions and chaos. Absolute terror was breaking out nationwide. Reports from Kharkiv, Chernihiv, Mariupol, Kyiv, and Lutsk made it seem like the whole country was under siege.

For the next week I barely slept. I was on the phone sixteen hours a day, early in the morning until late at night, checking in on staff, getting updates from our YWAM bases, and trying to manage the unending stream of calls and messages coming through. When I collapsed into bed at the end of the day, I still woke up every few hours to check in with Ruslan and make sure there were no bombs falling on Ternopil. For the girls and me, there was no time to talk or process. No time to think. Every moment was about doing all we could to help Ruslan, our family, our community, our home, Ukraine. Even when I had to drive somewhere, the girls would take turns reading me the messages and questions coming in and texting back my replies.

People called from everywhere, wanting to learn what I was hearing from the ground in Ukraine and asking how to help and where to send money. We quickly established giving sites through YWAM and local churches, as well as several circle teams. One of these circle teams was the Crisis Response Group, made up of YWAM leaders from the USA and Europe. Each member of this circle had a strategic responsibility aimed at getting information about the needs on the ground where our YWAM teams were operating. These needs from within Ukraine and on the border were continually changing, and our job was to get information to the people who could provide a response to those needs as quickly as possible. Many circle teams were deploying to the borders surrounding Ukraine to better assist the millions of refugees fleeing the country. Other teams were forming to prepare spaces on our YWAM bases throughout Europe to help house these incoming refugees.

I was called for interviews from KXLY News 4 in Spokane and Premier Christian Radio in the UK. Area churches asked me to visit. Even a journalist from South Africa reached out for an interview. I had never imagined I would experience another event like the Crimea crisis of 2014, but the 2022 invasion of Ukraine surpassed it by far in scope and intensity.

The war gave an immediate platform to all whose ministry was focused on Ukraine. We were called on to help the world understand why Russia was attacking Ukraine and to open doors for people to help. Most of all, we encouraged the church to pray. The world was outraged by the invasion, and many people were afraid the war wouldn't stop in Ukraine.

Then something extraordinary happened. Ukraine didn't surrender. Vladimir Putin thought it would be all over in seventy-two hours, but the people of Ukraine stood firm against an enemy vastly superior in number and weaponry. People of every village, town, and city rallied against the Russian army for trying to steal their land and liberty. Their bravery came to be seen as a David and Goliath story, a fight for freedom that inspired people around the world. I was deeply touched by the sight of homes and businesses in my home state flying the Ukrainian flag.

On February 27, four days into the invasion, I stood in front of the congregation of Lakes Community Church in Newman Lake, Washington. This felt like such an Esther moment. It was a "for such a time as this" opportunity to share a message of hope and explain the many needs, in this crisis that had captured the attention of the entire world. I looked out over an audience that was silent and still. Many of them were friends who had visited Ukraine on short-term mission trips over the years. I gave them an update on Ukraine and how our YWAM base was filled to the brim with refugees. I asked them to pray for President Volodymyr Zelensky and for a victory over tyranny. I also asked them to pray for the people of Russia, that they would have the courage to oppose the war and to finally break free from the stronghold of Communism that never truly lifted from their land.

In conclusion, I said, "I don't know what tomorrow holds, but I know who holds tomorrow. This battle belongs to the Lord. He goes before us. He is our rear guard. He will never leave us in this hour of great need."

In the first three months of the war, more than fifteen million Ukrainians fled across the borders of Poland, Hungary, Slovakia, Romania, and Moldova, a number unprecedented in world history. Refugees waited in lines ten to fifteen miles long trying to cross borders into Western Europe. The Russian invasion is the largest armed conflict on European soil since

World War II. Its aim is to terrorize a neighboring nation into submission. The situation was indeed terrifying, but Ukraine did not submit.

"The territorial defense came knocking on our door," Ruslan reported on one of our calls. "They asked if we wanted rifles to defend ourselves. I declined the offer, but it begged the question: What will we do if our city comes under attack?"

"I pray it never comes to that," I replied. "Babe, how long do you think this war is going to last?"

"I don't know," Ruslan said. "But for the first time in my life, I feel proud of my Ukrainian heritage. Ukraine will fight for its freedom, for the right to be their own country, whatever the cost."

As the first days of war turned into the first weeks, our little YWAM base became the humanitarian aid hub for our entire city, working directly with local churches and the mayor's office. Ternopil saw hundreds of thousands of refugees come through its doors. Refugees slept on the floors of train and bus stations, and churches unscrewed pews from their sanctuaries to make room for people to sleep. Our building, which on a normal day had twenty-six beds available, was making space for more than a hundred people each night. We offered refugees a safe place to sleep, some food, and an opportunity to stabilize before they continued their journey to the border.

Area restaurants brought food. Some days it was sushi and pizza; other days some of the fanciest restaurants in the city brought their best dishes to help YWAM feed the masses of people coming through our building. Our colleagues from YWAM Europe in Romania, Norway, Germany, Sweden, the Netherlands, and many other countries brought over vans and semitrucks full of food and humanitarian aid. We received so many supplies that we had to rent a warehouse to store them. As the war intensified, especially in towns near Kyiv, calls for evacuation assistance and humanitarian aid kept flooding in. As soon as YWAM Ternopil could fill a van with whatever was requested, our brave team of men wearing bulletproof vests would leave to deliver it.

One of my favorite stories started with a call Ruslan received the second week of the war. The call was from a maternity ward in a town outside Kyiv that was being bombed day and night. All the women and newborn babies were kept in a bomb shelter under the building, and they were desperate for supplies—formula, diapers, feminine products, and other things needed for mothers and babies after delivery. Ruslan said he would do his best to find the requested items even though he had no idea where he would get them. Products like these were scarce, as stores around the city were not receiving goods quickly enough to keep their shelves restocked. As Ruslan exited our building, a van from YWAM Romania drove up. A team had come with supplies and a desire to help for a few days. Ruslan opened the van's back doors and was stunned to see it was full of baby formula, diapers, feminine products, and almost everything else on his list. Instead of having to scour the city for these supplies, Ruslan simply received from this little team God's provision of everything needed.

It was truly amazing to see the way our community, and the communities around Europe and the world, found a way to work together to help Ukraine. In my estimation, Youth With A Mission was one of the first, foremost, and most effective organizations on the ground from day one, just doing the next thing, day in and day out.

Our workers, including Ruslan, were exhausted, but they kept going. They stopped only to go home before the curfew set in, and they were out the door as soon as it lifted. When the emotional weight of all he was hearing and seeing became too much, Ruslan would duck into the little cleaning closet on the first floor to cry. Indeed, all the men and women on our base had tearful moments during those days.

Our home was also full of refugees. Like a thrown-together family, ten to fifteen guests at a time often stayed in our home during the first months of the war. I was so thankful that our home could be a safe harbor for these people. It was such a silly thing, but I was glad for the day I had spent cleaning the house prior to our departure. I hoped the spring decor brought people a little bit of joy.

In the face of unfathomable needs, our family had been swept up in this mobilization of Christians to be the hands and feet and heart of Jesus to the Ukrainian people in this hour of terror and hardship. I have never experienced such a move of God as those first months of war. Every day my heart broke at the awful and terrible news coming out of Ukraine. And every day I marveled at the way God had mobilized the church around the world in prayer and service. Each day brought stories of battlefront horror, but also stories of miracles, protection, and provision. Those were the stories that kept me going.

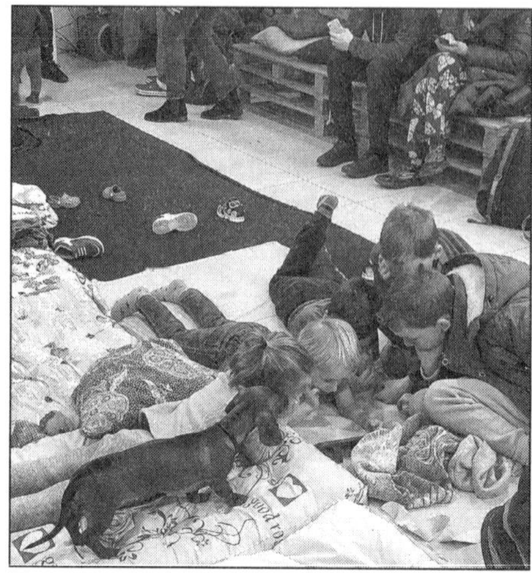

Left: Ukrainians taking refuge in the basement of YWAM Ternopil. Thousands of displaced Ukrainians spent the night during the first three months of full-scale war in Ukraine.

One of the YWAM Ternopil classrooms being converted into space for storing incoming humanitarian aid

Caravan: YWAM Ukraine staff and volunteers heading to the front lines to deliver humanitarian aid and rescue stranded Ukrainians in some of the most dangerous areas of the country during the first three months of the war

CHAPTER 21

Holding Tight to Jesus

As the first days of full-scale war unfolded, the girls and I lived each day not knowing what tomorrow held. We keenly felt the separation from Ruslan, and the desire to get back to Ukraine to help was powerful. Yet every minute, there was such a sense of God's presence and direction. One of our leaders likened our situation to building an airplane in flight. We were in motion, and each day there was a little more order to the chaos. For those of us who called Ukraine home, everything had changed. We were moving into new realities and new positions. When people would ask me how I was doing, I would simply say, "I'm holding tight to Jesus!"

This crisis felt different than what we experienced in 2014. We recognized a new kind of strength in us. The journey of brokenness in coming out of Crimea had made our family stronger as we faced this crisis. While we were still devastated, we had no doubt we could trust Jesus to see us through. There was peace and purpose in our hearts, and for the moment, that was enough. Jesus was holding on to me and the girls. He also was holding on to Ruslan, to our dog Mimi, to our home, to our friends.

During the whirlwind early weeks of the war, I could see that without a doubt, Jesus was holding on to my mother as well. He could, and would, work wonders for an elderly woman from northern Idaho while also working wonders mobilizing his people all over the world to help Ukraine.

About four days after our arrival in Idaho, I was able to visit my mom at her assisted-living community in Sandpoint. I was thrilled when I walked into her room and she called me by name. We had a sweet, sweet visit. We sang hymns together and looked through some of her books. I played with Mom's cat, Alley, then tidied up her apartment. I didn't talk about what was happening in Ukraine. I knew Mom wouldn't be able to understand anything I might have wanted to share. Still, just being together again brought me great comfort.

Later, at an appointment with the director of the assisted-living community and her assistant, I expressed how much I appreciated their concern for my situation and the care they had shown for my mom. After we had talked for a few minutes, the director explained that Mom's dementia had accelerated in the past year. "Everyone loves your mom," she said, "but she is coming into a season in which she needs more care than our community can offer. We ask that you arrange for her to move as soon as possible."

I was shocked. This was not at all what I had been expecting. But when the director explained the challenges they had with my mom's care, I could see that she did need more time and attention than they could provide. As I walked out of that meeting and got into my car, I just felt so overwhelmed.

Lord, really? Really! How am I supposed to deal with this on top of everything else? It's just too much.

As my frazzled brain began processing various options, a bit of revelation struck me. Yes, finding a new home for Mom, moving her, and helping her get settled did present a significant crisis for us. But I found it humorously comforting that, in comparison with the other crisis I was facing, this one did not look so bad.

Then I recalled how just a few hours earlier, Mom was singing her favorite song with me. "One day at a time, sweet Jesus. One day at a time."

Yes, Lord. Just one day at a time. That's how we'll get there. Suddenly, a clear and sure thought popped into my head. *Move Mom home.* It was a crazy idea, but the more I thought it over, the more I recognized this could be the answer. Home was the house my dad had built, the house I had grown up in. I considered how amazing it would be if I could move Mom back there, assisted by full-time caregivers. I had wondered many times if that might be possible, and in the past couple of years, we had begun the process of renovating the main floor of the house. We had also undertaken a great purging of the house's contents. It was possible that we could get the house ready to be a care facility for my mom. We just needed to find caregivers.

It would not be easy, but I felt in my gut that this was what the Lord was leading me to do. The biggest challenge in finding caregivers was the isolation of Mom's Priest Lake home. It was forty miles from the nearest town, fifty miles from the nearest hospital, and one hundred miles from the nearest large city. People I talked to said it would take a miracle to find qualified workers to care for Mom full-time. Well, I believe in miracles. I would do my part, and I would trust God to do what I couldn't. It would take at least two women to care for Mom full-time to get started, more as we developed the team further. But we would need to find these first two caregivers before the end of June, Mom's deadline for leaving her current apartment. Otherwise, the only other option would be to place Mom in a facility that specialized in memory care.

As I put the wheels into motion for what I hoped would be Mom's move home, the Lord began putting the girls and me into motion, repositioning us from Idaho to Poland to serve Ukrainian refugees as well as to set up a hub ministry that would offer support to our YWAM staff and volunteers. As we set off on this new assignment, I trusted that God was more than capable of caring for all his children at once—in Idaho, in Poland, in Ukraine, and everywhere.

Fast forward several eventful weeks (more about them later) and while working in Poland, I received an email from an eighteen-year-old woman named Dahlia Franey. She had been one of my campers at church camp in the USA a few years back. She had just received her nursing-assistant certification, and she wanted to talk to me about caring for my mom. The next day, I received another unexpected email from a seventy-eight-year-old woman named Inamae Henderson. She had been a caregiver all her adult life, and she also was interested in caring for my mom. Both women were believers, and both had outstanding references. Still, I wondered how I could put two women of such differing ages in charge of Mom. The timing of their emails seemed curious, though, and I wondered if this wasn't God putting together the miracle I had prayed for.

A week later, both Dahlia and Inamae said yes to moving in together to care for Mom. Neither of them agreed solely because they were in need of employment. In praying over the opportunity, each felt from God that my mother was their next assignment.

God had done the miracle I had asked him to do. He was moving my mom back home, providing two loving women to help take care of her. It was such a gift, such a blessing. It filled me with faith to hope harder for the miracles we so desperately needed in Ukraine.

Without a doubt, in every situation, we held tight to Jesus, and we could feel him holding tight to us.

Gloria and Emily with their grandma, celebrating Mom's November birthday early one year with a summer picnic near Sandpoint

CHAPTER 22

Ambassadors of Hope

Three weeks into the full-scale invasion, the girls and I were back on a plane heading for Kraków, Poland. We were so grateful to be traveling back in this direction, as supporting displaced Ukrainian people became such a priority for us. We didn't just want to be there; we needed to be there. The border was as close as Gloria, Emily, and I could get to home for now, since Ruslan still did not think it was safe enough for us to return to Ukraine. We hoped Ruslan could join us in Poland soon. It had already been more than a month since we had said goodbye to him in Ternopil. That month felt like something out of a World War II novel. Our family needed to get arms around each other and be all in the same place.

But for now, we were focused on the work we had come to do. As the Russia-Ukraine War intensified, refugees and aid workers were pouring into Poland. God was leading us to open a ministry center in Kraków to help support YWAM staff and volunteers based in Ukraine as well as those flying in and out of Kraków's John Paul II International Airport, the closest major air hub to Ukraine. Our ministry center would offer pastoral care and hospitality to aid workers and volunteers associated with our mission.

We soon started calling this location the Kraków Care Apartment, and we began to mobilize pastoral-care professionals. We were looking for people who could teach us crisis-management skills, coping mechanisms, and trauma care. We needed to learn what to ask and what not to ask as we helped aid workers process the impact of their experiences. I hoped this kind of care would make a difference in the longevity of our workers' service.

Our other objective was to help at refugee support stations along the Poland-Ukraine border. YWAM and international agencies such as UNICEF and World Kitchen were committed to helping the millions of Ukrainians fleeing the country.

Four days after our arrival in Poland, the girls and I connected with the YWAM team at the Medyka-Shehyni border crossing. Emily and Gloria were holding up amazingly well for young women just fourteen and seventeen years old. I wondered how all of us would cope when we began to engage with the waves of Ukrainian refugees coming into Poland. I could only imagine what they had suffered in their journey to get to the border.

YWAM managed two of the many aid tents set up at this border crossing. One was a place for refugees to rest awhile; the second was full of personal hygiene items that were available for free. Soon Emily and Gloria were at work helping to keep the "store" in stock or running to get tea or food for those who came into our tent to rest.

The refugees were not hesitant to share their stories. We soon realized that people needed to talk about what they had been through. Much of our time was spent simply sitting and listening. Our tent became not only a sanctuary for those who needed to rest, but also a place to unload some of the burden of what they had seen and experienced. Many had lost so much. I thought a lot about how I could comfort such people.

"Don't give up!" I would say. "There are good people in this world, and they want to help you." Other times I said, "You will find your way back to okay again. God is with you." I also asked, "Would you allow me to pray for you?" I used those sentences every day.

On one such day, I popped my head into the rest tent and noticed both my girls deep in conversation with an older couple.

"We came from Chernihiv," the man said. "The bombing was so terrible, we just couldn't stay another day."

His wife held a cat on her lap. "We brought with us what we could, but most important, we have our cat, Tom, with us."

As I stepped into the tent to say hello, the girls introduced me to Sergei and Svetlana, and of course Tom.

"I'm so glad you were able to bring your cat," Gloria said. "We have a dog named Mimi in Ternopil. I miss her so much."

As they continued to talk, Tom the cat suddenly jumped up and out of his collar and out of Svetlana's arms. Svetlana shrieked as her cat darted out of the tent. "I'm not taking another step ANYWHERE without Tom!" she declared.

As I watched this unexpected crisis unfold, the girls recruited volunteers to try to retrieve Tom. They tempted him with food. They called his name. They prayed. And finally, Emily was able to grab hold of one paw and pull the cat back into the arms of Svetlana.

We were in a camp surrounded by organizations that are deployed in crisis zones all over the world. These professionals have a million times more experience working in refugee camps and war zones. Yet it was two teenage girls who touched the hearts of this older couple. For a few hours that day they became like granddaughters, serving and listening and getting dirty rescuing a beloved cat.

That evening, as we went home, both girls informed me in very firm voices that serving refugees was where they were supposed to be. They did not want to leave. From that day forward, they were the first to jump out of their beds in the morning, throw on their orange YWAM Volunteer vests, and head off to be the answer to someone else's prayers.

As we continued our work along the border, Ruslan finally made it into Poland. We enjoyed a joyful, tearful reunion. The plan was for him to spend five days with us, then return to Ternopil. But five days later, when Ruslan tried to cross back into Ukraine, he was denied entrance. Because of wartime complications with traveling on his American passport, Ruslan would have to wait ninety days before he would be allowed to reenter Ukraine. This was a crushing blow, but as the weeks unfolded, Ruslan discovered he was also needed at the border, and it was such a gift to be together.

Over the next three months we positioned ourselves back and forth between Kraków and the Poland-Ukraine border. We bounced around from one temporary housing spot to another. It felt like everyone we had ever met in our YWAM career was making their way through Kraków down to the border and into Ukraine. We loved seeing them all. Often they would stop by our latest apartment or meet us for coffee in one of Kraków's many cafés. I soon began to look for vacation rentals with large living rooms and a full kitchen so that we could open our doors to the large groups that showed up for dinner.

The girls did their best, lugging their schoolbooks from one place to the next, and soon they found a few favorite coffee shops to get some schoolwork done each day. As always, the goal was to get back down to the border each weekend, where we felt such a burden for the refugees coming in.

As our first month in Poland turned into our second, we shifted our efforts from the border crossing to a refugee camp housed in a Tesco building in the Polish town of Przemyśl. If you can imagine a store like Costco in the USA being completely emptied of its shelves and all that empty space being turned into a refugee center, then that's exactly what this Tesco was. Run by volunteers from all over the world, it was the largest transitional refugee center near the Ukrainian border. Untold thousands of refugees came through its doors. Every day, buses full of Ukrainians were unloaded here, registered, given a place to rest, and offered medical care. Then came the big decision. Representatives from countries all over Europe as well as from nations including Israel, Canada, and Japan had come to invite Ukrainians to apply for refugee status in their country. Refugees could simply go country shopping, and once they chose which country they would go to, the representative would arrange for their travel and provide instructions for what to do on arrival.

Our family spent two months consistently volunteering at this location. Gloria and Emily especially became some of the most popular volunteers. Their expertise as interpreters and their willingness to work hard opened up a variety of opportunities for them to help. When they weren't being called on to translate, they were busy playing with children, babysitting pets, mopping floors, disinfecting cots, or spraying down sheets and bedding to keep bed bugs and lice at a minimum. There was no way to launder the bedding for the hundreds of people who came and went every day, so the goal wasn't necessarily to clean the sheets, but to sterilize them.

A woman from Britain named Tracy directed the area where our girls often worked, and she did her job from a wheelchair. It took about two seconds for us to realize that her disability in no way interfered with her ability to command her troops! She quickly directed people in what they needed to do and how to do it. Often there were questions or situations that required an interpreter. She could be heard from one end of the building to the next yelling, "Translator, I need a translator!"

On one such day, Emily was the first to answer the call for assistance. She found Tracy with a group of camo-clad American soldiers.

"Emily! There you are!" Tracy exclaimed. "We have new volunteers from the US military. I would like you to give them the tour, introduce them to some of the people in this area, and then show them how to properly disinfect the cots, stack them, clean the floors, and then arrange them again."

"Okay," Emily replied.

Gloria, who was working in a different area that day, looked up to see her fourteen-year-old sister walking by with the US military in tow. Emily was calmly explaining where all the cleaning supplies were and how to do the task of disinfecting the cots. To this day, it's one of our favorite stories of our time of service at the Tesco Refugee Center—Emily commanding the US troops.

Out of all of us, Ruslan spent the most time volunteering at this location. He was busy from morning until evening fixing things, greeting incoming refugees, helping carry luggage, answering questions, and just being a listening ear. One morning he arrived to see a woman standing by a pile of bags with a worried look on her face. He felt a nudge to see if he might be able to help her in some way.

"Hi," he said, "my name is Ruslan, and I'm one of the volunteers here. Is there anything I might be able to help you with?"

The woman looked Ruslan up and down and took a moment before she answered. "I need to use the bathroom. But I don't know what to do with all my things."

"I'd be happy to watch over them for you if you'd like," Ruslan offered.

The woman looked at him for a moment longer before answering. "I'm fifty-five years old, and everything I have left in the world is in those bags."

"Ma'am, I won't move an inch from your belongings until you are ready to take possession of them again," Ruslan assured her.

The woman sighed in relief. "In that case, maybe you wouldn't mind if I also took a minute to smoke my cigarette outside?"

Ruslan smiled. "Take all the time you need."

Without a doubt, the most important thing Ruslan did that day was to stand guard over this woman's worldly possessions.

Back in Kraków, we finally signed the lease on the Kraków Care Apartment in late April. It had taken almost six weeks to find a good location for the care apartment because thousands of Ukrainian refugees and aid workers were also looking for apartments to rent. We sensed that we would know the location when we saw it. And when Karen Armstrong, one of our beloved coworkers from YWAM Montana who had come to join our care team, found it, she knew it was the one.

The apartment had two bedrooms and two bathrooms with a living room that connected them. One of the bedrooms even had a bear-claw tub positioned in the middle of the room! The living room looked out over the little market square right in the center of Oldtown Kraków. We were told that it was exceedingly rare to find a long-term rental in such a location. It was located on Sienna 7, apartment 7. Just as God rested on the seventh day, we hoped many of our staff and volunteers would find rest at this location.

Between March and December 2022, more than eighty aid workers took advantage of the Kraków Care Apartment's respite program. While with us, they caught up on much-needed sleep, ate home-cooked meals deliciously prepared by our care team, met daily with a trauma counselor, and had time to enjoy one of the most beautiful cities in Europe. Many workers said this opportunity to process their own experiences and receive ministry themselves made the difference for them to be able to continue to serve during the war. I am so thankful for the more than thirty volunteers who served the Kraków Care Apartment at various times during those months.

The respite retreats came to an end in January 2023, but we continued to run the apartment as a hospitality center until April 2024. It was a place set apart for teams and individuals coming and going from Ukraine as well as for YWAM staff and volunteers in need of rest. It was a place to debrief or take a break. A place free of air-raid sirens and the constant threat of the next attack. A place to be reminded for a moment what life outside a war zone feels and sounds like. This location served hundreds of faithful missionaries working on the front lines of the war in Ukraine.

Meanwhile, alongside the launch of the Kraków Care Apartment, our family had continued our work with refugees. As spring 2022 turned into summer, we had stayed in more places than we could easily count. Someone asked me what I was missing the most, and I instantly replied, "My clothes, my closet, and my community." All of which were in Ukraine. I had literally been wearing the same clothes for sixteen weeks, the girls too. We were weary of living out of suitcases. But when tempted to feel sorry for myself, I reminded myself that in Ternopil I still had a closet, clothes, and a community. I had met hundreds of families who had lost all those things.

Amidst rolling blackouts, air-raid sirens, and untold casualties, the Ukrainian people continue to make their valiant stand against the Russian invaders. Meanwhile, our family flies back and forth over the Atlantic Ocean, traveling between Ukraine, Kraków, and north Idaho. I tell people all the time that while all of Ukraine is an active war zone, not all areas are as dangerous as others. Ternopil has been one of the safer areas, and we recognize that the gift of going to school, going to work, going to coffee, and falling asleep peacefully at night in these regions has come at a huge cost. Driving past the cemeteries across Ukraine, you see flag after flag after countless flag flying over the graves of Ukraine's fallen heroes. We look forward to the day when the millions of displaced Ukrainian families, including ours, can return to Ukraine full-time.

In the meantime, each of us takes our next step of faithfulness. Our daughter Gloria graduated from high school in 2023. At the start of 2024 she began her DTS in Lausanne, Switzerland, with her outreach in Egypt ministering to Sudanese war refugees. She is currently studying at Wheaton College outside Chicago. Our daughter Emily is in her senior year of high school at House of the Lord Christian Academy. She will graduate in the spring of 2025 and then also plans to head off on her DTS journey. Both have worked alongside us as we've served refugees as volunteer aid workers in the USA, Poland, and Ukraine. In the face of unfathomable needs, God has mobilized our family, alongside so many others, to be the hands and feet and heart of Jesus in many different locations and to a multitude of people. He has called our family to be ambassadors of hope for Ukraine.

We have now passed more than one thousand days of the Russia-Ukraine War. I don't know exactly how this story ends. I don't know the outcomes of the next battles. I don't know what world leaders will do. I don't know when the Borodins will live full-time again in our new house in Pidgorodne, or if our property in the Carpathians will one day host a retreat center for the workers God has filled with his love for Ukraine. Our story hasn't moved in the ways we expected. Instead of our children finishing their childhood in our new home, they are finishing it in the home where I finished mine, helping to take care of their grandma.

Since 2022 we have taken three deployments as a family back home to Ternopil and Poland, for a total of eight months. Being able to serve in our community during these months has been a great blessing for us as a family, as has continuing to open our home in Pidgorodne for staff gatherings, YWAM retreats, and special times together.

We are also encouraged that God is moving in the Carpathians, near our mountain property. In the fall of 2022, I helped the care team organize a care retreat for YWAM Ukraine staff and volunteers at a hotel venue near our Carpathian property. A short time later, one of our YWAM bases in Lutsk began a ministry called Renewal and felt led to use a hotel venue in this same area as their location. For more than a year now, every two months the staff put on a retreat for soldiers and their families. Some of these families still have loved ones fighting on the front. Some of the participants are wounded vets, some former POWs. At this beautiful location, soldiers and their loved ones have the opportunity to tell their stories, be ministered to, remember what it feels like to enjoy life together as a family, and find new starting places toward their healing as they move forward. The Renewal retreats take place just a short walk from our mountain property, and we are praying for the funds and the team to make this a permanent location for ministry to those most impacted by this war. Isn't it amazing that this vision and location we first started praying into eight years ago would be used in ways far beyond anything we could have imagined preparing for? Thank you, Jesus.

Jesus is the constant in this story. I have discovered that his faithfulness and leading over our lives has twists and turns and unexpected detours... and takes us to places we never thought we would be and through experiences we never expected to have. Yet he has taught us how to have joy and be expectant and dream even when he himself is only thing we know for sure is around the corner. He is more than enough.

My story—and perhaps yours—has been full of themes of displacement. It might be easy, reading our story, to wonder if God misplaced the Borodins—to wonder why we would be released into one thing, only to have crisis uproot us...twice. I have wondered that too. But I've come to think that our journey in this broken world is better described another way; I think the terms *repositioned* or *strategically displaced* better capture our story.

The impact of crisis and tragedy, often without a moment's notice, changes us and the course of our lives. For us, I believe that doors that had been so beautifully opened were closed when Putin made his choice to invade Ukraine. The goodness of God is that we weren't just lost or cast to the side at the whim of a madman in this season of political upheaval. God has always placed us somewhere else where we could continue the work he has called us to do.

Part of the miraculous move of God is that out of the chaos, God gives us a position in our repositioning. He gives us a strategy in our displacement. Bringing beauty out of ashes, God connects us to others and activates us to be the help to those around us. God's redeeming presence is there when we are ready to see it. It brings hope and purpose to the place we presently are, even as we pray and hope to return in some way to the places where we used to be. When you think about it, aren't we all strategically displaced? Our true home is heaven, and until we go there, God has a position, a strategy, and sure coordinates for our good and the good of others within his divine GPS.

Jesus holds our tomorrows. He is actively at work in our tomorrows. And right now, though our circumstances are often full of hard and horrible, he is present. He is good. He is faithful. We can trust him. What a relief that is.

When we are walking through the valley of the shadow of death, as it says in Psalm 23, the Good Shepherd is with us. And wherever he is, even in the most horrible place, something good will happen. The war in Ukraine is a good example of that. Somehow, amidst the ashes of the unspeakable is the sweet presence of our God. He is at work in the good and the bad. It's a journey of hope and horror, hallelujah and horrible, all mixed together. But isn't that the story of Christ? Hope and horror and hallelujah. We don't know all the details along the way, but ultimately, we know how the story ends. In victory.

During the first months of the war, I ran into a woman named April who had been on staff with YWAM in Ternopil back before our family came there. Since then, she has been working in some of the poorest and most remote jungle villages of Papua New Guinea. The missionaries there run a medical clinic and a small village church. She told me that when the war started, she was working at this village mission, and she was invited to speak about Ukraine during the Sunday-morning service. As the service ended, the congregation took an offering for Ukraine. They asked April to deliver these funds to be used to purchase medical supplies.

As April finished telling me this story, she handed me an envelope with two hundred dollars in it. "This is the offering from Papua New Guinea. They are praying for Ukraine."

These are the stories that move me to tears and fill me with hope. The body of Christ around the world is praying for Ukraine, even from the jungles of Papua New Guinea.

I pray that my story in turn has brought you hope, the sure hope that God is trustworthy and actively at work in and through our situations. I pray that all passersby of these pages will see how great and gracious our God is, to work out his beautiful redemptive story through our lives.

This story isn't over yet, the battle is still fierce, but it is well with our souls.

NGOs from all over the world came to provide support for the millions of Ukrainian refugees coming over the border into Poland, March 2022. Our YWAM tents are just to the right of the Ukrainian flag.

The girls volunteering at the Poland-Ukraine border crossing, offering free hygiene products to refugees passing through, 2022

The newly rescued Tom the cat with his mom Svetlana, a refugee from Chernihiv, in the YWAM rest tent at the Poland-Ukraine border, 2022

Ruslan helping transport a Ukrainian babushka along the Polish border crossing, 2022

Dozens of buses just like this one dropped refugees off daily at the Tesco Refugee Center in Przemyśl, Poland, 2022

Cots ready for the next bus load of Ukrainian refugees

Ukrainians could apply for refugee status in one of several countries. They would depart for these countries within one or two days.

Arms around Papa for the first time in a month!
So good to be together again.
March 2022, Rzeszów, Poland

The Borodin family, Switzerland, March 2024

AFTERWORD

A Call to Prayer

I hope you have enjoyed reading our story. I also hope that reading our story has helped you understand some of the context of Ukraine's fight for freedom. I hope it will inspire you to pray for this country that forty million people call home. All have experienced incredible loss because of this terrible war. Pray that their stories of death, destruction, and loss will not define us as a nation. I recently heard a colleague say that the five to seven years after a war has ended are actually worse for survivors than the war itself. Pray, even as we wait for Ukraine's liberation, that God would already be preparing the church for the nation's healing and restoration.

Pray for President Zelensky and his family. If ever there was a world leader who needed our prayers it is him.

Pray also for the people of Russia. Whether they all know it or not, they also are in a battle for their freedom. Pray that truth would break through and that many Russians will have the courage to stand against this evil time.

Pray for the heroes of YWAM Ukraine who have served steadfastly in such incredible hardships. I have never been so proud to be part of this mission and so proud of what God has released through it as I have been in this present season.

One of the themes of this book is my mother's dementia journey. My mom is doing well. When we aren't in Ukraine or Kraków, we live with her and her incredible team of caregivers. She doesn't know who we are anymore, but when she sees us, she knows we are people she loves. Spending five minutes in her presence is more precious than I can describe. Every day she showers us with words of blessing! "Oh, you're so beautiful! You're so wonderful! Bless your heart! I love you." Often after all her praises she finishes with a resounding "Amen!" It's an unexpected gift amidst the ongoing losses of dementia. Becoming the holder of your parents' memories is quite extraordinary. Watching them lose those memories, tragic. Some precious ones lose their ability to communicate early in their dementia journeys. Many lose their personalities long before their bodies give out. If you have someone in your life walking through the losses of dementia, whether patient or caregiver, lift them up in prayer, and maybe also take a moment to reach out and listen to some of their story.

Lastly, consider praying for those around you who might be walking through their own season of personal displacement and repositioning. You never know, but you just might be the answer to someone's prayer, in their greatest moment of need.